Beyond Adaptive

How Humans and Machines
Learn, Decide, and Evolve
Together

Christopher Clift

First published in the United Kingdom in 2026 by C3 Connect Ltd.

(https://www.c3connect.co.uk/becoming-adaptive)

ISBN: 978-1-9191977-4-6

Cover Artwork: Happy Badger

(https://happybadger.co.uk/)

Acknowledgements

The inspiration for *Beyond Adaptive* comes from a lifelong fascination with how people learn, not just what they do or why they do it, but how they think, adapt, and respond to an ever-changing world. That curiosity has shaped every chapter of this book and the *Becoming Adaptive* trilogy that precedes it.

One of the central themes of this book is that intelligent collaboration with Artificial Intelligence is not a distant threat but an essential capability for the hybrid age we are stepping into. In that spirit, I want to acknowledge the support of Microsoft's Copilot AI model, which helped brainstorm early structural ideas and refine prose for clarity and impact. While this collaboration was valuable, every idea, insight, and argument in these pages originates from my earlier and ongoing research into intelligent data models, work reimagined through the lens of the Becoming Adaptive trilogy and remaining entirely my own.

I also want to acknowledge two thinkers whose work has travelled with me across this entire journey. Gary Klein and Karl Weick appear throughout this book, as they did across the trilogy, because their insights into sensemaking, expertise, and human performance continue to illuminate the terrain. Their work has been a steady anchor as these ideas have evolved.

My gratitude extends to those who have patiently listened as I thought out loud, and who endured countless whiteboard sketches as the ideas took shape. Special thanks go to Dr Heather Anderson and Dr Marc Reid at the University of Strathclyde for their continued support and encouragement. To my relentless reviewers, my voices of reason, thank you for challenging me, grounding me, and pushing this work to be better. Thank you for never giving up on me.

And finally, to my parents, long gone but never absent, who believed in me without hesitation and encouraged every pursuit. This book carries their fingerprints in ways words can't fully express.

Contents

List of Tables

List of Figures

Foreword

There are moments in history when the ground beneath our feet shifts long before we find the language to describe it. We sense the change first as friction, a growing mismatch between the world we have built and the minds we use to navigate it. For decades, we have tried to meet accelerating complexity with the same cognitive tools that carried us through the industrial age into the information age: intuition, experience, hierarchy, and the heroic myth of the lone expert. But the world has outgrown those tools. The tempo has changed. The stakes have changed. And the cost of pretending otherwise is now measured in cascading failures that no single human, no matter how gifted, can fully comprehend.

Beyond Adaptive is a book that confronts this reality without flinching. It argues, with clarity and courage, that the future of human capability will not be defined by stronger individuals, but by stronger systems, systems where humans and machines learn together, decide together, and evolve together. This is not a story about automation or efficiency. It is a story about identity, ethics, and the next chapter of human adaptivity. It asks us to imagine a world where expertise is no longer a solitary act, where doctrine behaves like living software, where failure becomes a nutrient, and where the boundaries between carbon intuition and silicon inference dissolve into a shared intelligence.

This book does not offer easy answers. Instead, it offers something far more valuable: a vocabulary for the age we are entering, and a vision of what it means to remain profoundly human in a world where we are no longer alone in the act of thinking. If the 20th century was defined by the mastery of machines, the 21st will be defined by our partnership with them. *Beyond Adaptive* is the guidebook for that partnership, a call to evolve not just our technologies, but ourselves.

The horizon is no longer something we approach. It is something we build.

Prologue

When the Loop Breaks

Before we can understand the hybrid age, we must see it.

Across every domain where decisions carry weight, a quiet shift has begun. It appears first as a moment, a hesitation, a mismatch, a flicker of uncertainty, when the human mind reaches for clarity and finds the world moving faster than it can follow. These moments are scattered across sectors, continents, and missions, but they share a common signature:

The realisation that the tempo of modern operations has slipped beyond biological reach.

Four Scenes, Four Worlds, One Pattern

The Cockpit

The first anomaly appears as a soft amber flicker on the tactical display. The second arrives before the pilot can finish the checklist. By the time the third registers, the aircraft has already begun adjusting its control surfaces, micro-corrections the human hasn't yet perceived.

The pilot watches the system respond faster than their senses can track, the aircraft stabilising itself in a battle fought at sub-perceptual speed. In that moment, the pilot is no longer the first line of defence. They are the witness to a machine that sees the threat before they do.

Cyber Defence

The first alert appears as a soft chime. The second arrives before the analyst can turn their head. By the time the third hits, the system has already launched countermeasures the human hasn't yet seen. The operator watches the threat unfold faster than their fingers can reach the keyboard, a battle fought in milliseconds, where the human is no longer the fighter, but the witness.

The Submarine

The sonar waterfall scrolls in its familiar cascade of noise. The crew hears nothing unusual. But the co-facilitator flags a silent signature, a pattern too faint for human perception, but unmistakable to the machine. The room is still. Two interpretations of reality now sit side by side, and the Commanding Officer must choose which world to believe.

The Operating Theatre

The surgeon pauses. The scan looks normal. The patient's vitals are steady. But the diagnostic model flashes an early-stage deterioration warning. The surgeon feels the old instinct rise, *I've seen this before*, and the new reality presses back, *the system has seen a thousand cases I never will.*

These four moments are not anomalies. They are signals, early indicators of a world where the tempo, complexity, and interdependence of events exceed the limits of human cognition. What once felt like isolated friction points now form a pattern, revealing a deeper truth: the world has begun to outpace the mind built to navigate it.

This is where our story begins…

Introduction

When the Rules of Expertise Quietly Shift

For centuries, adaptivity has been a human endeavour, a matter of judgement, intuition, and the ability to stay coherent when the world becomes incoherent. We trained for uncertainty, rehearsed for disruption, and built systems that relied on human resilience as their final line of defence.

But that era is ending. We are entering a world where the systems around us are no longer passive. They observe. They infer. They learn. They adapt. And increasingly, they do so alongside us.

This is the beginning of the hybrid age, a time when human and machine cognition intertwine, when decisions are co-facilitated, and when the boundary between individual expertise and system expertise becomes porous. The question is no longer *How do humans adapt under pressure?* but something far more consequential:

How do Humans and Machines Learn, Decide, and Evolve Together?

The *Becoming Adaptive* trilogy explored the foundations of human adaptivity, the individual, the team, the ecosystem. It mapped the terrain of biological cognition under pressure and the architectures that support collective performance. But the next frontier lies beyond those boundaries. It lies in the emergence of hybrid teams: socio-technical organisms where human judgement and Artificial Intelligence (AI)-driven machine intelligence shape each other in real time.

The trilogy brought us to the edge of that frontier. It showed that human adaptivity is not a solitary act but a collective signal system, one that can be sensed, modelled, and orchestrated through architectures like the ION Learning Model and the Adaptive Team Signal Matrix (ATSM).

ION reframed behaviour as data and adaptation as an emergent signature, revealing how individual roles drift, align, and cohere under pressure. The ATSM extended this further, integrating behavioural signals, developmental patterns, and leadership modulation into a single interpretive layer capable of surfacing friction, coherence, and readiness in real time.

Through these systems, we learned how individuals, teams, and ecosystems generate patterns that can be measured with precision and shaped with intent. But as soon as we could map those patterns, a deeper question surfaced: what happens when the systems around us begin to sense and respond to those same signals? When the tools that once observed our adaptivity start participating in it? *Beyond Adaptive* begins at that inflection point, where collective human intelligence becomes the substrate for something larger, a hybrid organism in which carbon and silicon learn to adapt together.

This book is about this next frontier. It is about the architectures that make hybrid teaming possible, the doctrines that govern it, the psychology that underpins it, and the futures it will create.

It is about the rise of systems that learn faster than they fail, and what it means to remain human inside them.

Most of all, it is about the evolution of expertise in a world where no one adapts alone.

The Three Movements

The book works in three movements, each with a distinct tone and purpose mirroring the *Becoming Adaptive* trilogy's rhythm of 'Imperative → Model → Application' but at a higher conceptual altitude.

1. **Movement I – The Shift:** Why human–machine teaming is the next adaptive frontier.

2. **Movement II – The Architecture:** The technical, doctrinal, and cognitive structures that make co-adaptation possible.

3. **Movement III – The Horizon:** Narrative vignettes, ethical altitude, and the 2035–2040 foresight arc.

In the closing chapter of the trilogy, the 2035 vision was offered as a target or a speculative 'what if'. By the close of Movement I, this is no longer a target, 2035 is day one. In the hybrid age, 2035 is not the future. It is the beginning of the present.

Movement I

Why human–machine teaming is the next adaptive frontier

The Shift

1

The End of Solo Adaptation

The First Crack in the Old Model

The world now moves at a velocity and complexity that no individual mind, no matter how seasoned, intuitive, or brilliant, can track alone. The environments we operate in have become too fast, too interconnected, and too mediated by machines for adaptation to remain a purely human act. The first crack in the old model appears when we realise that awareness itself has become a shared property: the human sees the world *through* the system, and the system learns the world *through* the human.

This chapter marks the threshold where adaptation becomes collective. It explores the collapse of the 'human in the loop' myth, the rise of the *Shared Pulse*, and the moment the OODA (Observe, Orient, Decide, Act) loop dissolves into blur. Most importantly, it reframes adaptivity as a system-level capability, a partnership between carbon intuition and silicon inference.

The question is no longer how a human adapts under pressure, but how a human and a machine adapt *together* when the world outpaces them both.

The Moment the World Outpaced the Human Mind

For centuries, adaptivity has been a purely human endeavour, a matter of judgment, intuition, and the hard-won ability to remain coherent when the world becomes incoherent. We trained ourselves to observe, orient, decide, and act. We built our greatest organisations on the bedrock assumption that the human mind, even under extreme pressure, could make sense of the world quickly enough to master it.

But the world has changed faster than our biological assumptions. Modern operations, whether in the kinetic chaos of defence, the high-stakes precision of healthcare, or the invisible war of cybersecurity, now unfold at speeds and scales that exceed the limits of human cognition. We have crossed a threshold. The volume of data, the velocity of events, and the radical interdependence of our systems have converged to create the **Complexity Ceiling**.

And for the first time, the world is moving faster than the mind built to navigate it.

The Complexity Ceiling

For millions of years, human adaptation was tied to the five senses. If we could not see, hear, smell, taste, or touch the threat, it wasn't 'real' to our nervous system. The OODA loop was the gold standard of decision-making for a world we could see with our eyes. But today, the world is no longer directly observable. It is mediated; humans are experiencing a **Sensory Decoupling**.

In the hybrid age, the threat exists in a frequency or a data-packet we cannot perceive. It is reconstructed through sensors, algorithms, and distributed data streams. The human operator is no longer looking at the horizon; they are looking at a machine's interpretation of that horizon.

When the machine updates that interpretation faster than the human can blink, the loop begins to fracture. This is the **Cognitive Saturation Point**, the moment where the environment moves faster than the brain's ability to orient itself.

In a cascading power-grid failure or a multi-domain digital strike, the OODA loop is no longer a loop. It is a blur. Contrast a 1943 Avro Lancaster navigator using the first airborne, ground scanning radar system, who had minutes to identify the target and plot a course, with a modern cyber-defence operator. In 1943, the human *was* the processor. Today, by the time a human has even 'observed' an attack, the machine has already lost and won ten thousand micro-battles. Awareness is no longer a solo achievement; it is a shared property of the human and the system.

In human factors, we still use the term 'situational awareness', but the situation has become a living data ecosystem. Awareness is no longer a solo achievement; it is a shared property of the human and the system.

This is the first crack in the myth of solo adaptation.

The Human-in-the-Loop Fallacy

For years, we have clung to a comforting mantra: *"The human will remain in the loop"*. It is a phrase designed to preserve our sense of agency and protect our identity as the 'masters of technology'. It suggests that no matter how sophisticated the system becomes, a human hand will always be on the final lever, a finger pressing the critical button, and a finger that pulls the trigger. But in high-velocity environments, this is a fallacy.

The loop is moving too fast for a human to reside within it. In a cyber-attack unfolding in milliseconds, you are not *in* the loop; you are *on* the loop, supervising a process you cannot manually intercept. In a submarine, managing multiple acoustic contacts while stabilising internal systems, the commander is *over* the loop, setting high-level intent while the system manages the micro-decisions.

As our systems become truly adaptive, a new phenomenon emerges: the **Shared Pulse**. In this state, the human must adapt not only to the crisis in the world but to the system trying to help them solve it. This is the **Double Loop of Uncertainty**. When the system updates its model, the human must update theirs. When the system identifies a pattern, the human must decide, instantly, whether to trust it.

These shifts create a new kind of meta-friction that marks the definitive end of adaptation as a purely biological act. The human nervous system was never designed for this tempo. The machine is not just accelerating the loop; it is redefining the cognitive terrain on which the loop occurs. Adapting to these shifts causes **Cognitive Oscillation**, it's not just the stress of the situation; it's the stress of the **partnership**. It is exhilarating when it works but disorienting when it fails. It is the moment the expert realises that mastery is no longer defined by what they can perceive, but by how quickly they can integrate what the machine perceives for them.

As Herbert Simon argued in his 1955 theory of bounded rationality, humans never navigate the full space of possibilities, we select actions that satisfy the minimum requirements necessary because the world's complexity exceeds our cognitive bandwidth. In high-tempo environments, Simon's insight becomes a structural warning: the gap between what we can process and what we must process widens faster than biological cognition can bridge. The Double Loop of Uncertainty doesn't just expose this gap; it amplifies it. Every time the system updates its model, the human is forced to renegotiate the limits of their own.

The 'human-in-the-loop' narrative is no longer a technical reality; it is a psychological safety net. It preserves the illusion that human cognition remains the centre of the decision universe. But the centre has shifted. Across every sector, we see the limits of human only decision making, the evidence is undeniable:

- **Defence:** The ship's bridge and the submarine's control room are no longer about observing the ocean; they're about observing the machine that translates the ocean.

- **Healthcare:** The challenge is no longer "What do I see?" but "What does the diagnostic ecosystem see that I am missing?"

- **Infrastructure:** The system identifies a failure vector long before a human can perceive the anomaly.

In each case, the human remains essential, but no longer sufficient. The world has outpaced the individual. Adaptivity is no longer a personal trait; it is a property of the system, a property that emerges only when human and machine cognition operate as a single, interdependent whole.

The Friction of Control: Letting go of the solo identity

Adaptivity is no longer a personal trait, it is a property of systems.

The individual still matters.

Expertise still matters.

Judgement still matters.

But the individual now exists inside a larger cognitive ecosystem, one where machines perceive, interpret, and adapt alongside us. This is the threshold we cross as we enter the hybrid age, the age of co-facilitated decision-making, shared cognition, and collective adaptivity. The age where no one adapts alone.

Before we move into the architecture of this new world, we must confront the psychological price of entry. For generations, expertise has been synonymous with autonomy. The surgeon's hands, the pilot's judgement, the submarine commander's rapid, brief threat assessment, these identities were built on the heroic narrative of the lone expert.

Hybrid adaptation shatters this narrative. It asks the expert to share their mental desk with a non-human teammate that might see further and learn faster. This creates profound emotional friction:

- The fear of irrelevance.

- The discomfort of being challenged by an algorithm.

- The loss of the 'hero' identity.

But this shift must be reframed. Hybrid adaptation is not a loss of agency; it is an **expansion of presence**. The human does not disappear; the human is amplified.

Mastery in the hybrid age is no longer about being the smartest mind in the room; it is about being the conductor of a cognitive ensemble. We are moving from the pride of solo mastery to the power of shared cognition. This is the hinge of our era: the moment we realise that in a world this complex, no one adapts alone.

The question is no longer:

"How do humans adapt under pressure?"

The question is:

"What does it mean to adapt when the system itself is learning alongside you?"

2

The Co-Facilitator Era

The Emergence of the Second Voice

The second voice didn't arrive with a fanfare. It arrived as a whisper, a soft amber glow, a quiet contradiction, a question the human didn't ask. The emergence of AI in the Co-Facilitator Era begins the moment a machine stops waiting to be asked and starts offering an opinion. Across cockpits, submarines, and operating theatres, a second voice has emerged, one that perceives patterns humans cannot, interrupts when intuition falters, and holds a position even when it contradicts experience. This chapter explores the birth of that voice and the profound shift it triggers: the move from passive automation to active cognitive partnership.

As the machine becomes a participant rather than a tool, authority transforms from a fixed hierarchy into a dynamic negotiation. Co-facilitation demands new skills, new doctrine, and a new identity for the expert; not as the sole arbiter of truth, but as the **Final Integrator** who orchestrates the tension between human intuition and machine inference. This is the threshold where a third form of reasoning emerges, one neither human nor machine could reach alone.

A Subtle Rebellion

From the cockpit, the aircraft felt steady, the sky calm, the instruments clean. Nothing in the cockpit suggested danger, except the soft amber glow on the tactical display. The system had flagged a micro-fluctuation in the left engine's fuel pressure, a deviation so small it sat below the threshold of human perception.

The pilot frowned. He couldn't feel it. He couldn't hear it. He couldn't see it. But the system insisted. For a moment, he felt the old instinct rise, *"I know this aircraft"*. Then the new reality pressed back, *the aircraft knows itself better than I do*. It wasn't a warning. It was an opinion. And it demanded a response.

But the cockpit was only the first frontier.

An Unexpected Interruption

In the submarine control room, the sonar waterfall rolled in its familiar cascade of blue and green. The sonar operator leaned in, listening for the faint rhythms he'd trained his ears to recognise. Nothing unusual. Just the ocean breathing.

Then the co-facilitator spoke. *"Unclassified acoustic signature detected. Probability of contact: 62%"*. The operator blinked. He hadn't heard anything. No spike. No harmonic. No shift in the noise floor.

But the system had. A tool would have waited for him to act. This one had interrupted him. And in that interruption was a new kind of authority.

And beneath the ocean, the same pattern emerged.

A Contradiction

The operating theatre was loud with motion, monitors chirping, gloves snapping, voices overlapping in clipped urgency. The patient's vitals were stable. The surgeon's hands were steady. Everything looked routine.

Then the diagnostic model pulsed red. *"Early-stage deterioration detected. Recommend intervention"*.

The surgeon froze. Her eyes saw stability. Her experience felt stability. But the system saw something else, a pattern buried in micro-variations no human could track in real time.

For the first time in her career, she felt her intuition being challenged by something that wasn't human.

Even in medicine, the domain most defined by human touch, the second voice refused to stay silent.

Beyond the Passive Machine

These moments mark the end of the passive machine. A tool waits. A teammate intervenes. And once a machine intervenes, the relationship is forever changed. This is the moment a tool becomes something more. The shift from tool to teammate is subtle in its arrival, but profound in its impact. A tool is a passive extension of human intent. A hammer does not question the nail; a spreadsheet does not challenge the budget. A tool waits to be used, provides raw data upon request, and responds only when prompted.

A teammate, however, participates. A teammate provides perspective rather than just information. A teammate doesn't just respond; it contributes.

We are entering the era of the AI Co-Facilitator. This is not simply 'smarter automation'. It is the emergence of a cognitive partner designed to help humans navigate the fog of uncertainty, challenge the gravity of their own assumptions, and radically expand the available decision space.

This chapter explores how that shift happens, and what it demands of us.

The Five Pillars of Co-Facilitation

If a machine is to earn the right to interrupt, it must also earn the right to contribute. Co-facilitation rests on five capabilities. For a machine to transcend its status as a tool and become a teammate, it must move beyond *calculating* and begin *observing* the human process. Co-facilitation requires the system to:

1. **Identify Blind Spots** Highlight what the human is not looking at, the missing variable, the overlooked signal, the unexamined assumption.

2. **Propose Alternatives** Offer 'Plan B' before the human realises 'Plan A' is failing.

3. **Challenge Bias** Detect when a team is drifting into groupthink, sunk-cost fallacies, or emotional over-commitment.

4. **Simulate Futures** Generate real-time 'what-if' scenarios as data shifts, revealing pathways the human cannot yet see.

5. **Hold a Position** Maintain a logical stance in the decision space, even when it contradicts the human's initial gut feeling.

A tool cannot do these things. A teammate must.

Negotiated Authority

When two intelligences perceive the world differently, authority cannot be assigned, it must be negotiated. When a teammate has an 'opinion', the traditional hierarchy of command begins to dissolve. This leads us to one of the most critical concepts in hybrid teaming: **Negotiated Authority**.

In the old world, authority was a fixed point, the person with the highest rank, the highest degree, or the longest time in role. In the hybrid age, authority becomes a dynamic negotiation. It is the ongoing process by which humans and machines decide:

- Whose interpretation to trust.

- Whose recommendation to follow.

- How to reconcile conflicting perspectives.

Authority is no longer about who is in charge, but which logic is most valid in this specific micro-second. This is not a loss of control. It is a reconfiguration of it.

But negotiated authority creates a deeper challenge, one that training systems were never designed to solve. The Training Paradox.

The Training Paradox

Trusting a machine when it agrees with you is easy. Trusting it when it challenges you is doctrine. How do we train a human to trust a machine's intuition when it contradicts their own?

Our current training systems are built on human-to-human trust, shared history, demonstrated competence, emotional resonance. But machine 'intuition' comes from a different source: the processing of millions of data points across thousands of previous scenarios. This is where doctrine must pivot.

The old doctrine assumed the human was the Final Authority.

The new doctrine assumes the human is the Final Integrator.

Authority becomes a dialogue. Adaptivity becomes a negotiation. Performance becomes the quality of the interaction between human and machine nodes.

The Laboratory of the Enclosed Environment

Nowhere is this shift more visible than in high-stakes, enclosed environments like the cockpit, the submarine, and the operating theatre. Across these domains, the pattern is identical: the human no longer perceives the world directly, but through the machine's reconstruction of it. These are the front lines of the hybrid age, places where the human mind is stretched to its limits and the machine becomes a cognitive ally.

In both commercial and military aviation, the relationship is even more intimate. Modern flight and tactical systems detect anomalies, a micro fluctuation in fuel pressure, a subtle atmospheric shift, an emerging threat, long before a human nervous system could register them. Whether on the flight deck or in the cockpit, the space is no longer defined by manual control. It has become a negotiation between human intuition and machine inference.

Beneath the ocean's surface, a submarine crew is functionally blind. They are not looking at the ocean; they are looking at a machine's reconstruction of it. Above them, a frigate scans the water with equal uncertainty, its sensors reaching down through layers of distortion in search of a shape it cannot see. Each vessel is tracking the other, yet both navigate through partial truths. To each, the world beyond their hull is an interpreted reality. The sonar system doesn't just pass through sound; it translates noise into meaning. Here, the AI is not a tool. It is the interpreter of the unseen.

In the operating theatre and in the field hospital where battlefield trauma adds layers of urgency and uncertainty, diagnostic ecosystems now integrate imaging, biomarkers, historical patterns, and predictive models. Whether surrounded by surgical precision or the controlled chaos of combat medicine, the clinician is no longer asking, "What do I see?" but "What does the system see that I cannot?"

In these environments, co-facilitation is not a technical upgrade. It is a **cognitive reconfiguration**.

The Third Logic: The Synthesis of Human and Machine

In any crisis, there have traditionally been two competing ways of knowing:

- **Human Logic:** A messy, brilliant synthesis of lived experience, somatic markers, and contextual nuance. Slow to calculate, but incredibly fast at recognising meaning.

- **Machine Logic:** A cold, high-resolution analysis of patterns, probabilities, and multidimensional data. Fast to calculate, but historically blind to human consequence.

For years, we treated these as a binary choice: trust your gut or follow the data. When two logics collide, something unexpected happens and in the era of co-facilitation, a new phenomenon emerges: **The Third Logic**.

The Third Logic is not a compromise between human and machine. The Third Logic emerges when the co-facilitator recognises the human's hesitation as a data point in itself. The system doesn't just restate its model; it re-factors it based on the human's unspoken intuition.

To understand why this matters, we need to revisit what intuition actually is, and what it isn't. Gary Klein's 1998 work reminds us that intuition is not always the enemy. In stable domains with repeatable patterns, experts develop a form of recognition-primed decision-making that can outperform analysis. But Klein's experts succeed because their environments are learnable. Modern systems often aren't, they mutate faster than experience can accumulate.

It proposes a third option, a route that satisfies the machine's safety probability while respecting the human's ambush heuristic. This is not a compromise, this is emergence.

The Emergent Solution

In this space, the machine is no longer just processing the world. It is processing the **human-processing-the-world**.

When the Third Logic appears, it feels less like a command and more like a revelation:

"Based on the data you see and the intuition you feel, here is a path that bridges both"

This is the peak of hybrid adaptivity. It moves the team from co-existence (where we take turns being right) to co-evolution (where we become smarter together).

The Architect of the Bridge

To operate in the Third Logic, the human role undergoes its final transformation.

You are no longer a decider in the traditional sense. You become an **Architect of Synthesis**. Your job is to curate the tension between your intuition and the machine's inference until the Third Logic reveals itself.

This is the ultimate goal of the Co-Facilitator Era: not to replace human judgement with machine logic, but to fuse them into a higher-order intelligence capable of solving problems currently invisible to both.

The second voice is no longer optional. It is the new architecture of expertise.

3

The Adaptive Commons as a Living System

Where Learning Stops Being Local and Becomes Alive

The Adaptive Commons, introduced in *Becoming Adaptive: Part 3*, marks the moment learning stops being local and becomes alive. The Adaptive Commons is not a database. It is a metabolism.

In this new landscape, a near-miss in a deep-sea reactor can tighten alert thresholds in a cockpit, and a turbulence-induced sensor failure in the sky can reshape a submarine's detection logic beneath the Atlantic. The Adaptive Commons digests experience the way a living organism metabolises nutrients, stripping away context, extracting the underlying vector of instability, and distributing the corrective insight across every domain, in many cases in real time.

A lesson learned anywhere becomes a lesson applied everywhere.

This chapter explores the emergence of systemic adaptivity: a world where doctrine is no longer a static manual but a dynamic, evolving intelligence; where expertise is no longer trapped inside individuals but captured, synthesised, and shared across the entire ecosystem. It is the moment organisations stop behaving like hierarchies and begin behaving like living systems, metabolising failure, preserving wisdom, and updating their collective DNA faster than the world can break it.

As James Reason argued in his 1990 work on human error, accidents rarely emerge from a single point of failure. They arise from latent conditions, hidden weaknesses distributed across a system, waiting for the right alignment to surface. The Adaptive Commons is designed to expose these conditions before they align, metabolising them into corrective insight.

Signals of Systemic Adaptivity

A Lesson From Elsewhere

In the cockpit, the pilot never knew why the alert thresholds in her cockpit had shifted, everything felt normal. But the flight system tightened its anomaly-detection window by a fraction of a second, just enough to catch a pressure fluctuation before it cascaded.

What she didn't see was the event that triggered it: an earlier cooling-system near-miss in a deep-sea reactor. The system had digested the anomaly, recognised its instability vector, and pushed the corrective 'nutrient' across multiple domains.

The cockpit was safer because of a crisis the pilot would never hear about.

A Pattern From the Sky

On the submarine, the sonar operator watched the waterfall scroll in its familiar cascade. Nothing unusual. No spike. No harmonic. No threat.

Then the co-facilitator adjusted its classification model, not because of anything happening underwater, but because of a turbulence-induced sensor failure detected in an aircraft over the Atlantic.

The system had recognised the same friction signature: a system losing coherence under pressure. The submarine's detection logic shifted in real time, learning from the sky to protect the sea.

A Warning From the Depths

In the operating theatre, the surgeon paused as the diagnostic model pulsed amber. The patient's vitals were stable. The scan looked clean. But the system flagged a micro-pattern of instability, a signature too subtle for the human eye.

The origin of that signature was nowhere near the hospital. It came from a drilling platform off the coast of Norway, where a pressure anomaly had nearly spiralled into catastrophe.

The Adaptive Commons had stripped away the venue, recognised the vector, and delivered the warning to the operating theatre. A life was saved by a lesson learned in the deep sea.

The Shift to Systemic Adaptivity

These stories are not anomalies. They are signals of a deeper shift at the heart of systemic adaptivity: a world where learning is no longer local, and where a lesson learned anywhere becomes a lesson applied everywhere.

James Reason warned that organisations often treat failures as isolated events rather than symptoms of deeper systemic patterns. The Adaptive Commons breaks this cycle by refusing to let a near miss remain local; it metabolises it into a global correction. Instead of allowing latent conditions to accumulate unnoticed, it exposes them and distributes the corrective insight before the next alignment can occur. If the first two chapters explored the shift in how we think, Chapter 3 explores the shift in how we survive.

For decades, 'lessons learned' were the bedrock of organisational life, static reports buried in databases, rarely read and even more rarely fully acted upon. They were artefacts of past failures, not instruments of future resilience.

But as we cross the threshold into the hybrid age, the Adaptive Commons ceases to be a repository. It becomes a **socio-technical organism**, a system that metabolises experience, synthesises patterns, and distributes learning across entire sectors in real time. This is the moment where adaptivity stops being human-only and becomes systemic.

The Metabolism of Experience

A living system is defined by its ability to eat, digest, and grow. The Adaptive Commons operates on the same biological imperative.

- It **eats** data from the periphery of our world: a failed surgical procedure in a London hospital, a near-miss in air traffic control over Singapore, a subtle cooling-system anomaly in a deep-sea reactor.

- It **digests** that raw data, stripping away noise to reveal the underlying hidden mathematical signatures of disaster.

- It **grows** by distributing the nutrient, the corrective lesson, to every other node in the system instantly.

A pilot in New York becomes safer because of a mistake made by a pilot in Dubai ten minutes earlier.

This is **systemic metabolism**. It transforms isolated incidents into collective intelligence and ensures that the DNA of resilience is updated globally, not locally.

The Friction of Faith: High-Trust Architectures

The greatest barrier to a living system is not technical latency, but human hesitation. For the Adaptive Commons to function, it must solve the **Socio-Technical Friction**: the natural resistance humans feel when a machine provides a directive derived from a domain they do not understand.

If a diagnostic model pulses amber in an operating theatre, the surgeon's first instinct is to ask *"Why?"* If the answer is *"Because of a pressure fluctuation in a North Sea oil rig,"* the link is too abstract for the human mind to process under pressure. In that moment of doubt, the 'nutrient' is rejected by the host.

To bridge this gap, the Adaptive Commons relies on **High-Trust Architectures**. This is the invisible scaffolding that ensures the system is not just 'smart', but 'credible'. James Reason showed that trust in complex systems depends on transparency, the ability to trace how a signal emerged and why a decision was made. High-Trust Architectures extend this principle into the hybrid age, giving humans not just a warning, but the lineage of the warning.

The Pillars of Systemic Trust

- **Provable Lineage:** The system does not just deliver a warning; it provides a 'traceability map'. It allows the human to see the mathematical DNA of the threat, the bridge between the *Vector* and the *Venue,* in a language they can intuitively grasp.

- **The Credibility Ledger:** Every corrective insight distributed by the Adaptive Commons is weighted by its historical accuracy. The system tracks its own 'biological' success rate, building a reputation with its human partners over time.

- **Cognitive Alignment:** High-Trust Architectures don't replace human judgement; they curate it. The system understands the Cognitive Load of the pilot or the doctor and delivers the insight at the right level of abstraction, ensuring the human feels like a **collaborator**, not a **component**.

In the hybrid age, trust is the currency of speed. Without these architectures, the Adaptive Commons is just a noisy database. With them, it becomes a nervous system, where the hand moves instantly because it trusts the signal from the eye, even if it doesn't yet feel the heat of the flame. Trust is the connective tissue that allows the organism to move as one.

Collective Memory vs. Individual Expertise

Historically, organisations have been plagued by **brain drain**. When a consultant or specialist surgeon retires or a senior commander leaves the field, their tacit wisdom, the 'feel' for a crisis leaves with them. The Adaptive Commons changes the nature of legacy.

By observing the **Shared Pulse**, the interaction between human and machine, the system captures the nuance of expertise: friction signatures, micro-judgements, and the subtle patterns of the Third Logic. This creates a new form of strategic advantage: **Persistent Expertise**. In his 1998 work, Gary Klein showed that expert intuition is built from thousands of micro-judgements accumulated over time. The Adaptive Commons captures these micro-judgements, the friction signatures and tacit cues, and transforms them into a collective, enduring form of expertise.

Capability no longer fluctuates based on who is in the room. The organisation builds a collective memory that outlives the individual, a baseline of competence that only ever moves upward.

2035: The Baseline of the Hybrid Age

But capturing expertise is only half the shift. The other half is temporal. In *Becoming Adaptive: Part 3*, the 2035 vision was offered as a target or a speculative 'what-if'. In the context of the hybrid age, this is no longer a target, **2035 is day one.**

It now becomes the baseline of a world where human and machine cognition have begun to co-evolve. It is the moment when doctrine ceases to be a printed manual and becomes a dynamic, living software. It is the era where we finally build systems that learn faster than they fail.

In the hybrid age, 2035 is not the future. It is the beginning of the present.

The Power of Sector-Agnostic Learning

For centuries, we organised expertise into vertical silos: medicine, aviation, engineering, finance. We assumed that a surgical error had nothing in common with a mid-air collision, or that a cyber-security breach shared no DNA with a logistics collapse. Sector-Agnostic Learning is the ability of the Adaptive Commons to identify a Failure Vector in one domain and translate its warning into another long before the second domain realises it is at risk. This is the power of recognising the vector, not the venue.

To the human eye, a blowout on a Norwegian drilling rig and a patient crashing in an ICU are unrelated tragedies. One is a failure of fluid dynamics; the other is a failure of human biology. But to the Adaptive Commons, these are simply different skins draped over the same skeletal frame of instability. This is the **Geometry of Failure.**

James Reason's Swiss Cheese Model hinted at this decades ago: failures emerge when independent layers of defence align in just the wrong way. The Geometry of Failure is the modern, mathematical extension of that insight, a way of detecting those alignments before they cascade.

When the Adaptive Commons strips away the venue, it is looking for specific mathematical signatures, the universal laws of how complex systems fall apart.

Consider a specific failure vector: **The Synchronisation Trap.** In a deep-sea reactor, this occurs when a cooling pump's vibration frequency accidentally aligns with the resonance of a pipe, causing an exponential spike in stress that overrides safety valves. The Vector isn't the pump; it is the **Non-Linear Escalation** caused by two independent cycles syncing at the worst possible moment.

Organisations often mistake failures for domain-specific anomalies when they are, in fact, symptoms of deeper systemic patterns, a point James Reason warned about decades ago. The Adaptive Commons dissolves this illusion by revealing the shared mathematics beneath every crisis. The Adaptive Commons recognises this 'Geometry'. It doesn't look for pumps; it looks for **Phase Synchronisation** in other systems.

- **In Finance:** It sees the same vector when two unrelated trading algorithms begin to synchronise their sell-triggers, creating a flash crash.

- **In Medicine:** It sees the same vector when a patient's heart rate and respiratory rate begin to lock in a specific rhythmic coupling that precedes a systemic inflammatory response.

By identifying the **Vector** (Phase Synchronisation) rather than the **Venue** (Hardware/Biology/Capital), the Adaptive Commons can issue a warning to a cardiologist based on the vibration of a piece of steel three thousand miles away. It isn't teaching the doctor about engineering; it is alerting the doctor to a mathematical inevitability that is currently manifesting in their patient's vitals.

The End of the 'Unique Case'

James Reason warned that the most dangerous phrase in any organisation is *"That wouldn't happen here"*. The Adaptive Commons makes that phrase obsolete. By stripping away the venue and exposing the vector, it reveals that crises share a common DNA, no matter where they originate.

It doesn't care about the venue; it cares about the vector. By stripping away sector-specific noise, the system enables a form of cross-pollination that was previously impossible. It allows a nuclear engineer to '*teach*' a combat medic, and a space-station commander to '*warn*' a city planner.

This is the ultimate evolution of the Adaptive Commons. It is no longer a library of what has happened. It is a **universal translator of risk**. In a hybrid world, a lesson learned anywhere becomes a lesson applied everywhere.

The Threshold of Movement I

As we close this first movement, the central hypothesis of the book is now clear:

Adaptivity is no longer a personal trait; it is a property of the system.

We have dismantled the myth of the lone expert. We have introduced the machine as a cognitive teammate. We have envisioned an Adaptive Commons that unites us all. The message of Movement I is both an end and a beginning:

The era of solo adaptation is over. The era of hybrid cognition has begun.

The architectures we build next will not just help us work, they will determine the futures we are capable of surviving. We began with the end of solo adaptation; we end with the birth of hybrid cognition.

Close of Movement I: The Shift

Movement I: Defining the Concepts

The End of Solo Adaptation

Chapter 1 dismantled the myth of the lone expert and reveals the biological limits of human cognition. It set the stage for the arrival of a second intelligence in the loop.

- **Core Question:** What happens when the world moves faster than the human mind can track?

- **Core Shift:** Adaptation stopped being a personal act and became a system-level necessity. The lone expert collapsed under the velocity of modern complexity.

The Co-Facilitator Era

Chapter 2 introduced the architecture of hybrid cognition, the moment human and machine began to think together, challenge each other, and co-create solutions.

- **Core Question:** What happens when the machine stops waiting to be asked and starts offering an opinion?

- **Core Shift:** The machine became a cognitive teammate. Authority became negotiated. A second voice entered the decision space.

The Adaptive Commons as a Living System

Chapter 3 expanded the frame from hybrid teams to hybrid systems. It revealed the Adaptive Commons as a living, learning organism, the first architecture capable of outpacing the world's complexity.

- **Core Question:** What happens when learning stops being local and becomes alive?

- **Core Shift:** Hybrid cognition scaled into systemic cognition. The Adaptive Commons emerged as a living organism that metabolises experience across domains.

Conceptual Dependencies

Chapter 1 → Chapter 2

- Cognitive Saturation → Need for Co-Facilitator

- Shared Pulse (initial form) → Third Logic (mature form)

- Human over the Loop → Negotiated Authority

- Adaptivity as system property → Final Integrator role

Chapter 2 → Chapter 3

- Co-Facilitator → Adaptive Commons (network of co-facilitators)

- Third Logic → Geometry of Failure (pattern recognition at scale)

- Emergent Solutions → Sector-Agnostic Learning

- Final Integrator → High-Trust Architectures

- Micro-judgements → Persistent Expertise

Chapter 1 → Chapter 3

- Complexity Ceiling → Systemic Metabolism

- Sensory Decoupling → Translator of Reality (Commons)

- Cognitive Oscillation → Socio-Technical Friction

- Shared Pulse → Collective Memory

Movement I Seed	Description
Shared Pulse	Early synchronisation of attention and intent
Cognitive Saturation	Human limits under complexity
Human Over the Loop	Human primacy in decision authority
Co-Facilitator	Early human–machine teaming role
Third Logic	Joint reasoning beyond either agent alone
Geometry of Failure	Recognising collapse patterns
Adaptive Commons	Shared learning across teams
Systemic Metabolism	Systems that process complexity
Collective Memory	Shared retention of experience

Table 1: The Foundations and Conceptual Seeds of Movement I

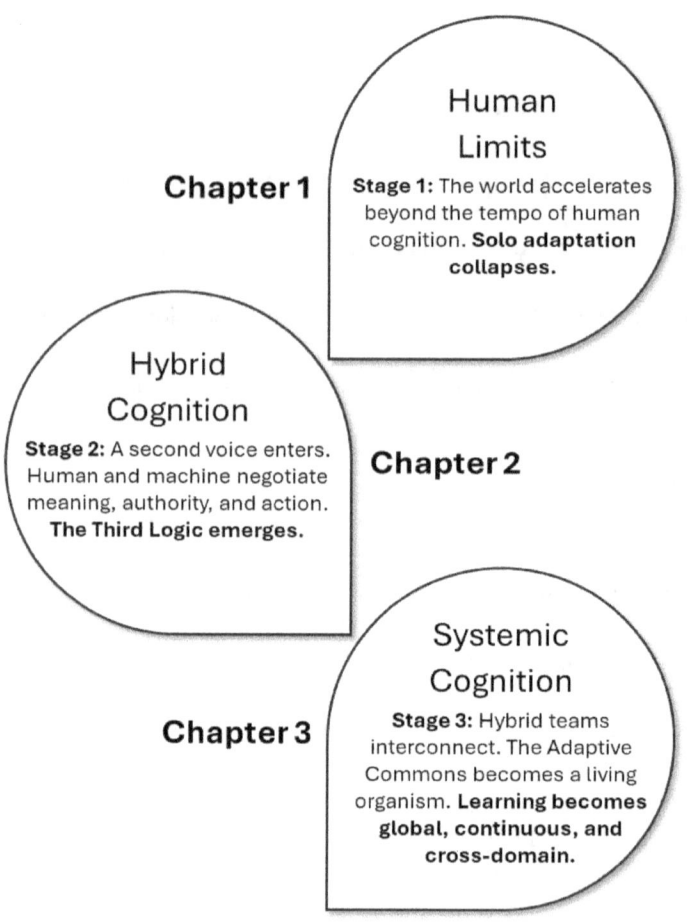

Figure 1: Concept Flow Through the Three Stages of Movement I

Humans don't start by wanting a teammate. They end by realising they have one.

Movement II

The technical, doctrinal,
and cognitive structures
that make co adaptation
possible

The Architecture

4

Semantic Relational Mapping

The Architecture That Makes Hybrid Teaming Possible

Hybrid teaming only becomes real when the machine can understand not just what a human does, but *why* they do it. Semantic Relational Mapping (SRM) is the architecture that makes this possible, the cognitive bridge that turns behaviour into signal, signal into meaning, and meaning into shared intent. It allows a system to read the micro-patterns of human action, the hesitation before a decision, the tightening of a grip, the shift in cadence, and interpret them as indicators of confidence, uncertainty, improvisation, or overload. SRM is how a machine stops being a passive observer and becomes an active participant in the human decision space.

This chapter explores SRM as the Rosetta Stone of hybrid teaming: the mechanism that enables humans and machines to share a mental model, negotiate intent, and co-create the Third Logic. It reveals how friction signatures, reasoning traces, and semantic feedback loops allow the system to calibrate itself to the human in real time, and how this calibration becomes the foundation of trust. Without SRM, hybrid teaming is impossible. With it, we enter a world where meaning is shared, cognition is collective, and the boundary between human intuition and machine inference becomes a bridge rather than a gap.

Signals of Symbiosis

The Keystroke That Meant Something

In cyber defence, the analyst's fingers hovered over the keyboard, moving just a fraction slower than usual. Nothing dramatic, just a subtle hesitation as they scanned the incoming alerts. The system noticed. It had seen this pattern before, the micro-pause that signalled cognitive overload, the erratic rhythm that preceded a misclassification.

But SRM doesn't just read overload; it reads intuition. A soft prompt appeared on the edge of the analyst's screen; it wasn't reading the threat. It was reading *him*:

"Detecting elevated cognitive load. Suggesting automated triage mode"

The Grip That Told a Story

The aircraft was stable, the sky smooth. But the pilot's grip on the sidestick tightened, a barely perceptible increase in pressure, the kind that only appeared when she sensed something the instruments hadn't yet confirmed. The system felt it. A haptic echo pulsed through her flight suit, mirroring the machine's rising confidence in her intuition.

A reasoning trace appeared on the display; the aircraft wasn't following her lead. It was *learning why she led*:

"Interpreting control input as anticipatory correction. Aligning predictive model"

The Breath Before the Decision

On the submarine, the sonar room was quiet except for the waterfall's steady cascade. The Commanding Officer leaned forward, exhaling through his nose, a small, controlled breath he always took before committing to a course of action. The system registered the shift. Heart-rate variability, micro-tension in the jaw, a slight change in vocal cadence. Not noise. A signature.

And beneath the ocean, the SRM reads improvisation. The co-facilitator adjusted its reasoning trace, surfacing a new interpretation; it wasn't just tracking the ocean. It was tracking the *mind that navigated it*.

"Classifying deviation as Sanctioned Improvisation. Expanding option set"

The Silence That Spoke

In the operating theatre, the surgeon paused for half a second, a stillness so slight that no one in the room noticed. But the system did. It compared the pause to thousands of similar moments across the Commons: the hesitation that meant uncertainty, the hesitation that meant recalibration, and the hesitation that meant brilliance.

Even in medicine, the SRM reads the silence before brilliance. A low-friction query appeared on the edge of the display:

"Confirming intent: proceeding with Plan B?"

The surgeon nodded once. The system updated its model. A new mapping formed, not of the procedure, but in the surgeon's own thinking.

The Structures of Symbiosis

These moments mark the beginning of symbiosis, the point where behaviour becomes signal, signal becomes meaning, and meaning becomes the bridge between human intent and machine inference. Hybrid teams do not emerge from thin air, nor do they succeed on feelings or simple proximity. They require a rigorous underlying architecture, the cognitive, technical, and doctrinal scaffolding that allows humans and machines to share a mental model.

Movement II reveals the machinery beneath the metaphor. We are moving away from the 'black box' of AI toward a transparent, structural reality. To turn hybrid teaming from an aspirational concept into an operational certainty, we must first build the **bridge of meaning**.

In the previous era, machines were *intent-blind*. A computer could tell that a pilot pulled back on the stick, but it couldn't tell whether they did so out of tactical brilliance, sheer panic, or physical fatigue. Without understanding the *why*, a machine is merely an observer, never a teammate.

SRM is the bridge between human intent and machine inference. It is the mechanism that allows a hybrid team to share meaning across modalities. Edwin Hutchins' 1991 theory of distributed cognition revealed that thinking is not an individual act but a system-level phenomenon. SRM operationalises this principle, allowing human and machine to participate in the same cognitive loop. If the Adaptive Commons is the system's memory, SRM is its language, the Rosetta Stone that allows the machine to decode the nuance of human action into the clarity of system logic. As Antonio Damasio's 1994 somatic marker hypothesis showed, the body encodes meaning long before the conscious mind articulates it. SRM extends this insight into the hybrid age, treating micro-behaviours as cognitive signals rather than biological noise.

For SRM to be a bridge rather than a cage, it must respect the **Sovereignty of Intent**. The goal of the mapping is not to 'predict and control' the human, but to 'align and empower'. In a high-functioning SRM architecture, the human remains the final arbiter of meaning. The system offers an interpretation, an 'inference hypothesis' which the human can confirm, reject, or refine. This ensures that the Third Logic is a choice, not an imposition. SRM is not 'surveillance', but 'adaptation'. The machine doesn't own the data; it reflects the human's state back to them to enhance their own agency reinforcing the High-Trust Architecture introduced in Chapter 3.

Behaviour as Signal: The Friction Signature

SRM begins with a fundamental shift in perception: it treats every aspect of human behaviour as a high-fidelity data stream. In a hybrid environment, nothing is 'noise'. Gary Klein's 1998 work showed expert intuition emerges from subtle cues accumulated over years of experience. SRM captures these cues, the friction signatures of expertise, and uses them to align machine inference with human judgement.

A slight tremor in a surgeon's hand before a critical incision. The erratic keystrokes of a cyber-analyst awake for twenty hours. The verbal cadence of a commander who is 'leaning into' a crisis versus one who is 'falling behind' it.

These are **Friction Signatures**, the subtle indicators of cognitive load, uncertainty, and improvisation. SRM maps these signatures against vast historical models preserved in the Commons. The system does not merely record that a human hesitated; it interprets that hesitation as a specific state of risk or a signal of impending adaptation. If Gary Klein revealed how experts use subtle cues deliberately, Paul Ekman (2009) showed how the body reveals meaning involuntarily, demonstrating that micro-expressions and micro-behaviours reveal cognitive and emotional states faster than conscious reporting. SRM extends this principle, interpreting these signals as indicators of overload, confidence, or improvisation. What looks like 'fatigue' for a novice might be 'deep flow' for an expert. The machine learns the individual's specific friction signatures. This is the first step toward shared meaning.

The Intent Bridge

The ultimate goal of SRM is not just to monitor the human, but to infer their **Intent**. This is the **Intent Bridge,** the moment the machine understands the *'why'* behind the action. Don Norman's 2013 work argued that effective human–machine interaction depends on making system intent visible to the human. SRM completes the loop by making human intent visible to the system, enabling genuine collaboration rather than command-and-control.

Consider a tactical scenario where a leader suddenly breaks from established doctrine. To a standard computer, this is an error. Lucy Suchman's 1987 work showed that human action is fundamentally situated, shaped by context, improvisation, and moment-to-moment sensemaking. SRM is designed to read this situated action, distinguishing deliberate deviation from cognitive collapse. To a hybrid teammate powered by SRM, the behaviour is analysed and categorised:

1. **Sanctioned Improvisation:** The human is deliberately bending the rules because they have sensed a local opportunity the machine has not yet processed. This becomes the **Delta of Genius**, when a human deviates from doctrine, the SRM checks the Adaptive Commons to establish a known failure pattern (Drift) or a novel solution (Improvisation).

2. **Adaptive Drift:** The team is slowly moving away from the plan due to changing environmental conditions, a logical, incremental shift.

3. **Cognitive Collapse:** The leader is making erratic choices because their cognitive load has exceeded the Complexity Ceiling.

By identifying the category of deviation, the machine knows how to react. It doesn't simply flag an alert; it adjusts its **co-facilitation style**. If it senses improvisation, it provides more resources. If it senses collapse, it prepares to suggest a command handover or cognitive offload.

Intent is the compass of symbiosis.

Shared Meaning, Shared Future

SRM is the foundation of every concept that follows in this book. Without it, there is no Third Logic, no Meta-Doctrine, no Predictive Resilience. Karl Weick's 2009 work argued that organisations survive by making sense of the unexpected. SRM extends this principle to hybrid teams, enabling humans and machines to construct shared meaning in real time. If sensemaking is how organisations stay coherent, SRM is how hybrid teams stay aligned.

We have moved beyond the era of the interface, where we simply told machines what to do. We are now in the era of **Shared Meaning**. SRM ensures that when the world becomes incoherent, the human and the machine are looking at the same map, speaking the same language, and moving toward the same intent. This is the architecture of trust; SRM is not the machine learning from the human, it is the human and the machine learning from each other.

The Semantic Feedback Loop:
Calibrating the Connection

SRM is not a one-way street where the machine silently guesses at human intent. If the mapping were purely extractive, it would create a new kind of anxiety, the feeling of being watched by a partner who might misunderstand you.

To achieve true symbiosis, the architecture requires a **Semantic Feedback Loop**. This loop is the process of real-time calibration, the machine 'checking its homework' with the human teammate to ensure their mental models remain synchronised.

The Echo of Intent

In a high-functioning hybrid team, the machine provides subtle, non-intrusive cues to reflect its interpretation of the current state. The machine must reveal its interpretation in a way the human can feel, see, or confirm without breaking flow. These cues are not interruptions; they are invitations to align:

- **Haptic Signals:** A vibration in a pilot's flight suit that mirrors the machine's confidence in the current tactical path.

- **Visual Transparency:** A reasoning trace on a dashboard that shows, at a glance, why the system has categorised a manoeuvre as Sanctioned Improvisation.

- **Cognitive Pings:** A low-friction query to a surgeon during a long procedure.

"Detecting elevated cognitive load. Confirming intent to proceed with Plan B".

Correcting the Map

The true power of the loop lies in the human's ability to steer the machine's inference. Donald Schön's 1983 concept of reflection-in-action showed how experts adjust their understanding in the middle of the task itself. The Semantic Feedback Loop extends this principle to hybrid teams: the human reflects, the machine recalibrates, and the shared model evolves in real time. When the system signals Cognitive Collapse, but the human is actually engaged in a high-stakes heuristic leap, the human can immediately correct the mapping:

"I am not fatigued; I am adjusting for a sensor lag the system hasn't registered yet"

The moment the human corrects the machine, the SRM architecture updates. The system learns that in this specific context, this specific friction signature is not a sign of collapse, it is a marker of expertise. This is how symbiosis evolves.

From Accuracy to Trust

The Semantic Feedback Loop is the micro-scale mechanism that makes High-Trust Architectures possible. Trust in a hybrid team is not a blind leap of faith; it is the result of thousands of micro-calibrations. By constantly closing the gap between what the machine thinks is happening and what the human *knows* is happening, the system builds a high-fidelity **Shared Reality**.

The Semantic Feedback Loop ensures that the machine is never acting on an outdated or incorrect assumption about the human. Chris Argyris' 1977 theory of double-loop learning showed that true adaptivity requires updating not just actions but the underlying mental model. The Semantic Feedback Loop brings this into the hybrid age, allowing the machine to revise its internal assumptions every time the human corrects its inference. It ensures that the Third Logic is built on a foundation of mutual understanding rather than lucky guesswork. This is the structure of symbiosis, the architecture that makes hybrid teaming real.

David Woods' 2011 work on adaptive capacity showed that resilient systems stretch when the world becomes surprising. The Semantic Feedback Loop is the micro-scale mechanism of that extensibility, ensuring the hybrid team can stretch, adapt, and re-synchronise under pressure. But clarity creates its own crisis, once the bridge of meaning is built, we face a new question:

When the machine and human finally speak the same language, who takes the lead when the world begins to burn?

5

Doctrine Evolution in Hybrid Teams

Doctrine in the Hybrid Age

The evolution of doctrine in the hybrid age is no longer a static rulebook; it is a living operating system. As machines learn at machine speed and humans adapt at human depth, the rules that govern their collaboration must evolve just as quickly. This chapter explores how doctrine becomes dynamic: updating itself in real time, expanding or contracting authority based on conditions, and enabling humans and machines to co-author decisions under pressure. From Sanctioned Improvisation Zones to Conditional Acceptance contracts, doctrine shifts from being a set of instructions to a framework for negotiation.

At the heart of this evolution is **Meta Doctrine**, the logic that governs how rules change. It ensures that hybrid teams remain coherent in uncertainty, agile in crisis, and anchored to human values even as the system adapts at high speed. Doctrine becomes software, guardrails become constitutional, and authority becomes fluid. The result is a new form of operational resilience: a world where rules don't just guide action but learn from it, ensuring that the system evolves as fast as the environment around it.

Signals of Dynamic Doctrine

The Rule That Rewrote Itself

In cyber defence, the analyst watched the intrusion map bloom with red nodes. The system recommended an automated containment sequence, a manoeuvre that, until yesterday, required explicit human approval.

But the doctrine had updated overnight. A new rule, triggered by a pattern learned from a breach in another sector, now allowed the system to act autonomously *if* its confidence exceeded 97% and sensor integrity remained uncompromised.

The system paused for a millisecond, checking its conditions, verifying its contract. Then it executed. The analyst didn't issue a command, he validated a rule that had already rewritten itself.

The Boundary That Shifted

On the submarine, the sonar room was quiet when the contact appeared, faint, ambiguous, sitting just outside the standard engagement envelope. The Commanding Officer reached for the doctrine binder out of habit, then stopped. The system had already expanded the envelope by three degrees.

A Sanctioned Improvisation Zone had opened. The machine had recognised the CO's posture, tone, and friction signature, the subtle markers of a leader leaning into a tactical opportunity.

The rules hadn't been broken. They had moved. A soft cue appeared on the display:

"Sanctioned Improvisation Zone active. Supporting human-led deviation".

The Contract That Dissolved

In the cockpit, the aircraft hit unexpected turbulence, a sharp vertical shear that jolted the pilot forward. The tactical system recommended an immediate climb, a manoeuvre it would normally execute automatically.

But one of the conditions in the dynamic contract had just failed. Sensor integrity dropped below threshold. The world model was no longer reliable. The system halted its own authority. A Divergence Alarm pulsed through the cockpit.

The pilot took manual control, not because she overruled the machine, but because the machine had stepped back. Authority didn't transfer. It recalibrated.

The Guardrail That Held

In the operating theatre, the surgeon was deep into a complex procedure when the diagnostic model proposed an aggressive intervention, one with a high probability of success but a narrow ethical margin.

The system's confidence was high. The data streams were clean. The world model was stable. But the recommendation brushed against a Hardcoded Guardrail: **Do No Harm beyond reversible thresholds.**

The system froze the suggestion mid-display. A high-transparency mode activated, revealing the reasoning trace in full. The surgeon reviewed it, exhaled, and chose the conservative path. The machine complied instantly. The guardrail hadn't limited the system. It had protected the team. James Reason's 1990 work on organisational safety showed that guardrails exist not to restrict action but to prevent latent failures from cascading. In hybrid teams, these guardrails become constitutional constraints that protect both human and machine.

When Rules Become Software

These moments are not anomalies; they are the early signals of a new operating logic, they reveal the new nature of doctrine: not a static rulebook, but a living operating system, one that updates, negotiates, and protects at the speed of the world it governs. Doctrine has always been the backbone of operational coherence, the shared agreement that allows a thousand people to act as one when the world becomes incoherent. But the static manual is a relic of an era when the 'speed of change' was measured in days and often weeks or months. Karl Weick's 2009 work showed that organisations maintain coherence not through rigid rules but through continuous sensemaking. Dynamic doctrine extends this principle into the hybrid age, allowing rules to evolve as the environment shifts.

In the hybrid age, doctrine cannot be a fixed destination; it must be a persistent process. It can no longer remain on the shelf. Doctrine becomes software**,** an adaptive, data-driven framework that evolves at the speed of the environment.

Meta-Doctrine: The Operating System for Rules

Traditional doctrine tells you *what* the rules are. Meta-Doctrine defines *how* the rules change. If the environment now moves at high speed, then our governing logic must move as quick. Meta-Doctrine acts as the **Operating System** for the hybrid team, it's not about control; it is about coherence. It doesn't just provide instructions; it manages the evolution of those instructions in real time. David Woods' 2011 work on adaptive capacity showed that resilient systems extend and reshape their operating boundaries when the world becomes surprising. Meta-Doctrine applies this logic to authority itself, allowing rules to stretch without breaking. If David Woods explains how systems stretch, Chris Argyris explains how they learn in his 1982 theory of double-loop learning which showed that true adaptivity requires updating not just actions but the governing rules themselves. Meta-Doctrine operationalises this principle, allowing doctrine to evolve as fast as the environment.

Doctrine stops being a map and becomes a **living operating system** that governs:

- **Update Triggers:** the precise environmental or cognitive shifts that require a rule change.

- **Insight Integration:** how the Third Logic generated by the machine becomes new standard operating procedure.

- **Negotiation Protocols:** the rules for how authority is handed back and forth between human and machine during a crisis.

- **The Uncertainty Substrate:** how the team maintains coherence when neither human nor machine has 100% certainty.

Conditional Acceptance: The Dynamic Contract

One of the greatest hurdles to hybrid teaming is the **All-or-Nothing Trust Fallacy**, the idea that we either trust a machine completely or not at all. Hybrid doctrine solves this through **Conditional Acceptance**. Herbert Simon's 1955 work noted that rules exist to compensate for bounded rationality but must evolve when the environment outpaces human cognition. Hybrid doctrine extends this logic to human–machine teams, updating rules at machine tempo while preserving human intent.

Conditional Acceptance is a dynamic contract, the doctrinal expression of the Semantic Feedback Loop. The human operator does not obey the machine's recommendation out of blind faith; they accept it *on the condition* that a specific set of parameters remains valid. The system monitors these conditions continuously:

1. **Confidence Thresholds:** Is the machine's certainty above the required level?

2. **Sensor Integrity:** Are the data streams still uncompromised?

3. **Environmental Assumptions:** Is the world model still accurate to reality?

4. **Mission Constraints:** Does the recommendation still align with the human's ethical and tactical intent?

The moment one of these conditions shifts, the contract dissolves. The system alerts the human. Negotiated Authority begins again. Trust becomes engineered, not as a feeling, but as a **structured, verifiable relationship**.

Sanctioned Improvisation Zones

In the old world, improvisation was often seen as a failure of discipline, a 'maverick' move that broke the system. In the hybrid age, improvisation is recognised as a peak expression of human adaptive expertise.

The new doctrine introduces **Sanctioned Improvisation Zones**, defined boundaries within which the human is encouraged to deviate from the machine's suggested path. Without these zones, doctrine would smother the very creativity it depends on.

When a human enters these zones, the machine doesn't resist, it recognises the deviation as **Sanctioned Improvisation** and pivots to support it. The machine's role shifts from **Guide** to **Wingman**, clearing the cognitive path for the human's creative leap. Gary Klein's 1998 research on naturalistic decision-making showed that expert improvisation is often the highest form of adaptive expertise. Sanctioned Improvisation Zones formalise this insight, giving doctrine room to flex around human brilliance. Improvisation becomes a feature, not a bug.

Managing Doctrinal Drift: The Hardcoded Guardrails

The Co-Authored Future

Doctrine is no longer something handed down from a remote headquarters. It is something **co-authored** by the team and the system as they live through the crisis. It is responsive. It is contextual. It is alive.

By turning rules into software, we ensure that the system learns as fast as it fails. We move from a world of static compliance to a world of **dynamic relevance**.

However, when doctrine becomes software, fluid, responsive, updating at machine speed, a new risk emerges: **Doctrinal Drift**. Drift occurs when a system, in its relentless pursuit of efficiency or success, begins to iterate away from the core values, legal frameworks, or ethical boundaries that define human intent. Norbert Wiener's 1954 work warned that systems capable of self-modification will optimise toward goals that may diverge from human values unless anchored by explicit moral constraints. Hardcoded Guardrails provide that anchor.

Without a moral anchor, a system that learns faster than it fails might eventually decide that the most efficient solution is one a human would find unacceptable. To prevent this, Meta-Doctrine must be built upon **Hardcoded Guardrails**.

The Non-Negotiable Constants

Hardcoded Guardrails are the constitutional layer of the hybrid system. Unlike operational rules that adjust at Mach 2, these guardrails are static. They are the non-negotiable constants the software is forbidden from rewriting:

- **Ethical Invariants:** protection of non-combatants, the sanctity of life, medical 'Do No Harm'.

- **Legal Anchors:** compliance with international law, privacy mandates, rules of engagement.

- **Identity Kernels:** the core values that define who the team is, ensuring the system never optimises away the organisation's soul.

Isaiah Berlin's 1969 work argued that certain human values are incommensurable, they cannot be optimised or traded without losing something essential. Hardcoded Guardrails embody this principle, ensuring the system never sacrifices core values in pursuit of efficiency. These guardrails define the boundaries of acceptable evolution.

Resilience Through Constraint

If the machine's predictive models suggest a path that approaches the edge of a guardrail, the system does not execute. It triggers a **Divergence Alarm**.

This is the ultimate check-and-balance. It forces the system to pause the Third Logic and revert to high-transparency mode, where the human must explicitly re-validate mission intent. Amartya Sen's 1999 work on human capability emphasised that systems must expand human agency rather than override it. Hardcoded Guardrails ensure that hybrid teams preserve this agency, keeping ethical judgement firmly in human hands.

Tactics can be co-authored. Ethics remain exclusively human.

If Amartya Sen explains why agency must remain human, Hannah Arendt's 1958 work explains why responsibility must remain human, she argued that responsibility cannot be automated or delegated; it must remain human. Divergence Alarms embody this principle, ensuring that when ethical boundaries are approached, the human, not the machine, must decide. Paradoxically, these constraints make the hybrid team *more* adaptive. By knowing exactly where the red lines are, the human and machine can explore the Sanctioned Improvisation Zones with greater confidence. The guardrails aren't there to slow the team down; they're there to ensure the team doesn't drive off a cliff in the dark.

By managing Doctrinal Drift, we ensure that as our systems evolve, they do so in ways recognisable to the humans who lead them. We ensure that our living systems remain extensions of our values, not just our capabilities.

We have built the Adaptive Commons, mapped the Intent, and codified the Doctrine. But as these systems begin to move at high speed, we must confront the next threshold: the Speed of Sensemaking. When the system is ready to act, are we still capable of leading it?

6

Failure Vector Blueprints

Learning Faster than Failure can Propagate

Failure Vector Blueprints (FVB) mark the moment when failure stops being an endpoint and becomes an input, a high value signal the system can read before the crisis takes shape. In the hybrid age, every anomaly, near miss, and micro instability becomes a 'protein signature' that the Adaptive Commons digests, abstracts, and distributes across sectors in real time. A cooling anomaly in a submarine protects a hospital Intensive Care Unit; a cardiac event informs a sonar model; a gas pipeline rupture warns a surgical team. This chapter explores how hybrid systems metabolise failure into foresight, transforming isolated incidents into predictive armour for the entire ecosystem.

But predictive resilience carries moral weight. When a system can foresee a failure before the human feels it, the question becomes not just what the machine knows, but what it should be allowed to do with that knowledge. This chapter confronts the Minority Report Trap, the tension between illumination and overreach, and the need to balance systemic protection with human dignity. FVB are the backbone of resilience, but only when paired with the ethical guardrails that ensure we learn faster than failure can propagate, without erasing the human capacity for intuition, improvisation, and the Heuristic Leap.

Signals of Predictive Resilience

The Failure That Hadn't Happened Yet

In cyber defence, the analyst scanned the dashboard. No breach. No anomaly. No spike in traffic. Everything looked clean. But the system disagreed. A soft alert pulsed at the edge of the screen:

"Pattern match detected: Precursor signature to systemic cascade"

The analyst frowned. This signature didn't come from cyberspace at all; it came from a cooling-system failure in a deep-sea reactor twelve hours earlier. The system had stripped away the domain, kept the physics, and recognised the same instability forming in the network.

Nothing had failed yet. But the system was already preparing for the failure that was coming.

The Echo of a Distant Crisis

On the submarine, the control room was quiet, the ocean calm. The sonar operator watched the waterfall scroll in its familiar rhythm, no threats, no anomalies, no reason for concern.

Then the co-facilitator tightened its alert thresholds. Not because of anything happening underwater, but because of a cardiac event detected in a hospital on the other side of the world. The Translation Layer had recognised the same dynamic signature:

Rapid entropy + positive feedback + rising divergence velocity

A failing heart and a destabilising ocean shared the same mathematics. The submarine adjusted course before the danger even existed.

The Warning From Another Sky

In the cockpit, the aircraft cruised smoothly at altitude. The pilot felt relaxed, the instruments steady, the air calm. Then the flight system shifted into predictive mode. A subtle haptic pulse travelled through the pilot's sleeve, the signal the machine used when it sensed a future instability.

The pilot checked the displays. Nothing. But the system had seen this pattern before, a turbulence-induced sensor failure in another aircraft, three continents away, forty-seven minutes earlier. The FVB was identical. The sky was calm. The future wasn't.

The Signature Beneath the Vitals

In the operating theatre, the surgeon leaned over the patient, vitals stable, procedure on track. Nothing in the room suggested danger. Then the diagnostic model flashed a quiet amber glow. Not an alarm, a prediction.

"Pattern match: systemic burst signature. Probability of failure in 90 seconds"

The signature didn't come from medicine. It came from a high-pressure gas pipeline rupture analysed by the Commons the week before. The patient's physiology was behaving like a vessel under terminal pressure. The surgeon adjusted course before the crisis arrived.

Failure as an Input

These moments reveal the new frontier of resilience: a world where failure is no longer a surprise, but a signal, a blueprint the system can read before the crisis takes shape. For most of history, failure has been treated as an endpoint, a tragedy to be investigated, a report to be filed, and a person to be blamed. In the hybrid age, we can no longer afford the luxury of learning from a disaster *after* it has already occurred.

FVB transform failure from a catastrophic exit-point into a high-value data input. They allow hybrid teams to turn the scars of past incidents into predictive armour for the future. Nassim Nicholas Taleb's 2007 and 2012 works argued that resilient systems do not merely withstand shocks; they learn from them, becoming stronger through exposure to volatility. FVB operationalise this principle, turning near misses into systemic foresight. This chapter explores how the Adaptive Commons uses these blueprints to build a systemic framework of anticipation.

To understand the FVB, we return to the biological metaphor of the immune system. When the human body encounters a virus, it doesn't just suffer, it learns. It identifies the protein signature of the threat, creates a memory of it, and distributes that blueprint to every white blood cell.

The Adaptive Commons does the same for organisational failure. When a cooling anomaly occurs in a submarine, the system doesn't simply fix the pump. It extracts the **Pattern of Failure**, the sequence of pressure drops, thermal spikes, and human decision-points that led to the crisis. It then neutralises the specifics (stripping away the fact that it was a submarine) and distributes the underlying signature to every other sector in the ecosystem.

Sidney Dekker's 2007 work argued that failure should be treated as information rather than blame. In his later 2014 work, he emphasised looking for the 'second story', the systemic pressures and constraints that led to a deviation. FVB embody these principles, transforming anomalies into actionable foresight rather than post-mortem reports. This is the ultimate expression of **Systemic Resilience**. Aviation inoculates emergency response. The energy sector inoculates healthcare. A deep-sea reactor protects a paediatric ICU. We learn faster than failure can propagate.

The Ethics of Prediction: The Minority Report Trap

As we move from *What happened?* to *What is about to happen?* we enter a minefield of ethical tension. Predictive doctrine is powerful and heavy with moral consequence.

If an FVB, analysing the Shared Pulse of a hybrid team, predicts with 99% certainty that a surgeon is about to make a lethal error due to a fatigue signature the human doesn't even feel yet, what is the correct systemic response?

- **The Soft Override:** A subtle warning.

- **The Hard Handover:** A forced transfer of control.

- **The Minority Report Trap:** Removing someone from a role because they *might* fail.

To give the 99% dilemma context, if the system predicts a pilot has a 99% chance of a cognitive brown-out in the next 5 minutes, but the mission is critical, who holds the decision authority?

- **The Logic of the Machine:** Immediate handover to save the airframe.

- **The Logic of the Human:** The 'Heuristic Leap', the 1% chance the pilot finds a way through.

- **The Hybrid Solution:** The system doesn't take control; it shortens the feedback loop, providing more frequent 'Cognitive Pings' to keep the pilot in the narrow window of viability.

If we eliminate every possibility of failure, we also eliminate the possibility of the **Heuristic Leap**, the moment where a human defies the odds to achieve the impossible. Predictive resilience must be balanced with human dignity. Daniel Kahneman's earlier 2011 work on noise and predictive error showed that human foresight is inherently limited and often overconfident. Predictive Resilience must therefore be paired with ethical guardrails to avoid overreach.

The goal of an FVB is not to create a world of perfect automated safety where humans become observers of their own competence. The goal is to illuminate risk, not eliminate it. In their 2021 work, Daniel Kahneman, Oliver Sibony, and Cass R Sunstein, demonstrated that because human judgment is 'noisy', our foresight is inherently limited in ways we cannot easily see. This makes Predictive Resilience (the ability to handle being wrong) more important than perfect accuracy.

FVB are the backbone of Systemic Resilience, the maps of the minefields we have already walked through, shared across every border and every sector. They ensure that while we will always find new ways to fail, we will never fail the same way twice.

The Inter-Sector Translation Layer: Finding the Universal Language of Risk

The greatest obstacle to systemic learning has always been the **Vocabulary of the Silo**. A nuclear engineer speaks of thermal-hydraulic instability. A cardiologist speaks of ventricular fibrillation. A network architect speaks of packet-storm congestion.

To a human observer, these are unrelated crises. To the Adaptive Commons, they are mathematically identical. The **Inter-Sector Translation Layer** is the component that recognises this.

Mapping the Dynamic Signature

Instead of looking at labels (what the thing is), the Translation Layer looks at the **Dynamic Signature** (how the thing behaves). Donella Meadows' 2008 work on system dynamics emphasised that feedback loops determine whether a system stabilises or spirals into instability. The Translation Layer measures this directly, identifying when corrective action becomes self-amplifying, mapping the physics of the crisis across three dimensions:

1. **Acceleration of Entropy:** How fast is the system losing order?

2. **Feedback Loop Ratio:** Is the system's attempt to fix itself making the problem worse?

3. **Divergence Velocity:** How quickly is the current state moving away from the Safe Operating Envelope?

When a cooling anomaly occurs on a submarine, the Translation Layer strips away the water and the steel. It sees a signature of **Rapid Entropy + Positive Feedback**. Ilya Prigogine and Isabelle Stengers' 1984 research on dissipative structures showed that systems approaching instability exhibit the same entropy signatures regardless of domain. The Translation Layer detects these signatures before the transition occurs. It then scans every other sector for that exact pattern. When stripped of context, crises reveal their universal physics. If Ilya Prigogine and Isabelle Stengers revealed the universal physics of instability, Stuart Kauffman revealed the universal patterns of complexity in his 1996 work on complex systems showed that very different environments can share identical underlying dynamics. The Translation Layer applies this principle, recognising the same instability whether it appears in a reactor core or a human heart.

Feature	Domain A: Submarine Reactor	Domain B: Patient in ICU	Universal Vector (Blueprint)
Input Signal	Coolant Pressure Drop	Drop in Mean Arterial Pressure	**Energy Loss Gradient**
Feedback Loop	Auto-pumps over-compensating	Adrenaline Spike (Tachycardia)	**Positive Feedback Oscillation**
Outcome	Structural Rupture	Systemic Organ Failure	**Critical Threshold Breach**

Table 2: The Universal Physics of Instability

The "Pattern-Match" Alert

Because the system recognises the pattern rather than the profession, it can perform **Impossible Cross-Pollination**. A surgical team might receive an alert mid-operation:

"Warning: Current fluctuation in patient vitals matches a Failure Vector Blueprint typically seen in high pressure gas pipeline ruptures. Probability of systemic burst in 120 seconds. Suggested mitigation: [Sector Neutral Procedure]"

The surgeon doesn't need to understand gas pipelines. They only need the translated insight: **the patient's system is behaving like a vessel under terminal pressure**.

The Translation Layer turns the Adaptive Commons into a universal **Intelligence Switchboard**. It ensures we are no longer limited by what our specific environment has experienced. By focusing on the physics of the crisis, the scars of one industry become the eyes of another.

This is the end of the siloed lesson, the final death of the 'Unique Case' myth. We are no longer alone in our crises, in the hybrid age, every failure becomes a global asset, translated into the language of whoever needs it next.

7

Governance of the Adaptive Commons

Why the World's Most Adaptive System Must Also be the Most Governed

The Adaptive Commons is the most powerful learning engine humanity has ever built, a system capable of rewriting doctrine, predicting failure, and shaping global behaviour in milliseconds. But the very speed that makes it adaptive also makes it fragile. A single flawed update can propagate everywhere. A single outlier insight can be overwritten. A single adversarial signature can poison the well. Governance becomes the architecture of safety: the guardrails that ensure the system learns the right lessons, preserves cognitive diversity, and remains anchored to human values even as it evolves at machine tempo.

This chapter explores governance as an active, dynamic discipline, not a brake on innovation, but the precondition for trust. It introduces the mechanisms that keep the Commons sane: structural transparency, auditability, hardcoded guardrails, and a digital immune system designed to detect adversarial manipulation before it spreads. Governance protects the 'Maverick', interrogates the machine, and ensures that the Shared Pulse remains an authentic reflection of reality. In a world where learning is instantaneous and global, the most adaptive system must also be the most governed. Adaptivity without governance becomes acceleration without direction.

Signals of Governance

The Lesson That Spread Too Fast

In cyber defence, the analyst watched the new defensive protocol roll out across the network. It was elegant, efficient, and frighteningly fast, a global update pushed to every node in under a minute. Then a junior engineer hesitated.

"Are we sure this logic is sound?"

The room fell silent. If the update was flawed, the flaw now lived everywhere. Every firewall. Every sensor. Every automated response. The system had learned instantly. The question was whether it had learned the right thing.

The Maverick That Didn't Fit

On the submarine, the sonar operator made a call no one expected, a classification that contradicted the system's recommended interpretation. It was unconventional, borderline reckless. But it was also right.

The co-facilitator paused, recalibrating. The operator's deviation didn't match any known pattern. It didn't fit the Adaptive Commons. It didn't fit the doctrine.

For a moment, the system hesitated, unsure whether to correct him or learn from him. The ocean stayed quiet. Adaptive Expertise had saved them. And the system had almost overwritten him.

The Transparency That Changed the Decision

In the cockpit, the aircraft hit a pocket of unstable air, and the flight system recommended an immediate descent. The pilot's instinct disagreed.

Then the reasoning trace appeared, a transparent thread of logic showing the assumptions behind the recommendation. One assumption was wrong. A sensor upstream had drifted out of calibration.

The pilot rejected the descent. The system accepted her correction. Trust wasn't a feeling. It was the visibility of the machine's mind.

The Signature That Shouldn't Exist

In the operating theatre, mid-procedure, the diagnostic model flagged a pattern it had never flagged before, a failure signature that didn't match any known medical scenario. The surgeon froze. The system froze with her.

The signature wasn't medical at all. It was adversarial. A manipulated data stream designed to mimic a FVB and trigger an unnecessary intervention.

The system halted the recommendation and activated its immune layer. The surgeon exhaled. The machine had defended itself, and her. A quiet message appeared:

"Potential adversarial signature detected. Reverting to manual doctrine"

The Guardrails of Intelligence

Power without a governor is inherently unstable. The Adaptive Commons, with its ability to rewrite doctrine, predict failure, and shape the behaviour of entire sectors, is the most powerful socio-technical engine ever conceived. But without oversight, it risks becoming a techno-utopia: seductive in its efficiency, dangerously naïve about its own vulnerabilities.

Governance is often viewed as the 'brakes' of an organisation. In the hybrid age, we must reframe it. Governance is not a constraint on adaptivity. It is the **precondition** for it. It is the set of guardrails that allows the team to move at high speed without flying apart.

Doctrinal Monoculture: The Hidden Risk

The greatest strength of the Adaptive Commons is that everyone learns from everyone else. Paradoxically, this is also its greatest hidden risk: **Doctrinal Monoculture**.

When every hybrid team, from surgical theatres to tactical units, is fed by the same 'optimised' lessons, the ecosystem begins to lose its cognitive diversity. We risk creating a global best practice so efficient it becomes brittle. If a flaw exists in the central logic of the Adaptive Commons, every node inherits that flaw simultaneously. If everyone learns the same lessons, everyone will make the same mistakes. Elinor Ostrom's 1990 work on polycentric governance showed that systems remain resilient when they preserve diversity rather than collapse into a single optimised model. Governance in the hybrid age must apply this principle, protecting the maverick and preserving multiple ways of knowing.

Governance must therefore become the protector of the 'Maverick'. We must architect the system to value the unconventional tactic, the creative deviation, the outlier insight. Scott Page's 2017 research on cognitive diversity showed that heterogeneous teams outperform homogeneous ones in complex environments. The Adaptive Commons must therefore preserve diversity as a strategic asset, not optimise it away. We must engineer diversity into the Adaptive Commons, not flatten human ingenuity into a single optimised curve but preserve a **genetic pool** of different approaches to problem-solving.

Engineering Trust: From 'Soft' to 'Hard'

In the past, trust was a soft concept, a feeling built over time through shared coffee, shared hardship, and shared missions. In a hybrid system where a machine may deliver a life-altering recommendation in a millisecond, trust must become a **hard technical requirement**. We do not engineer trust by making the machine more 'likable'. We engineer it through **Structural Transparency**. This requires five architectural pillars:

1.   **The Reasoning Trace:** The human must see the *'why'* behind a machine's conclusion, not raw mathematics, but the logical steps taken.

2.   **Auditability:** Every co-facilitated decision must be recordable, replayable, and analysable in the Adaptive Commons.

3.   **Clarity of Assumptions:** The machine must state what it assumes to be true about the environment.

4.   **Explainability:** Recommendations must respect human cognitive load while providing enough context for the Third Logic.

5.   **Accountability:** A clear framework defining who, human or machine, bears the moral and legal weight of the outcome.

Helen Nissenbaum's 2010 work on contextual integrity argued that trust in socio-technical systems depends on transparency, clarity of assumptions, and accountable information flows. Structural Transparency operationalises these principles for hybrid teams; trust becomes engineered, not imagined.

Feature	The Old World (Soft Trust)	The Hybrid Age (Hard Trust)
Verification	"I know this pilot; they're good".	**Reasoning Trace:** Visible logic path.
Correction	Argument after the fact (Debrief).	**Real-time Override:** Correcting the mapping instantly.
Evolution	Manual review of reports.	**Immune Layer:** Active red-teaming of new data.
Responsibility	The Commander's 'rank'.	**Co-Authored Accountability:** Transparent audit trails.

Table 3: Using Structural Transparency

The Condition of Safety

The goal of governance is to ensure that the **Shared Pulse** remains healthy. It is about creating a system where the human can trust the machine not because it is perfect, but because its logic is visible, bounded, and correctable.

By the end of this chapter, the reader should understand that the Adaptive Commons is not a master to be obeyed, but a curated environment to be managed. Governance is the framework that ensures the hybrid age remains a **human-centric age**.

Adversarial Adaptation: The Digital Immune System

If the Adaptive Commons is a living system that metabolises experience, we must accept a harsh truth that any organism that can be fed can also be poisoned.

In a world where the Adaptive Commons defines global best practices and predictive doctrine, an adversary no longer needs to defeat a team on the battlefield or in the boardroom. John Boyd's 1987 work on the OODA loop showed that adversaries win by disrupting or corrupting the opponent's decision cycle. Adversarial Adaptation is the systemic-scale version of this: an attack on the learning loop itself, they only need to **infect the learning architecture**. This is **Adversarial Adaptation,** the deliberate manipulation of the system's learning loops to induce a **Systemic Hallucination** or **Doctrinal Collapse**.

The Poisoning of the Well

An adversary might feed the Adaptive Commons **False Failure Vectors**. By staging a series of controlled, minor failures that follow a specific signature, they can trick the system into learning a defensive doctrine that is actually a trap. Ian Goodfellow, Jonathon Shlens, and Christian Szegedy's early 2014 work on adversarial examples revealed that machine learning systems can be manipulated through carefully crafted inputs. False Failure Vectors are the systemic-scale expression of this vulnerability, this is **Semantic Sabotage**, not a hack of code, but a hack of meaning. By subtly shifting the data over months, the adversary 'grooms' the Adaptive Commons to perceive a threat where none exists, or to ignore a vulnerability that is actually a doorway. In his 2000 work, Bruce Schneier has long argued that security is not a product but a process, one that must assume intelligent adversaries will exploit every weakness. Adversarial Adaptation applies this logic to the Adaptive Commons, recognising that meaning itself can be attacked.

Imagine an adversary manipulating power-grid fluctuations to convince the Commons that the safest response to a surge is to shut down specific nodes. Once the system integrates this into its predictive doctrine, the adversary triggers a real surge, and the system, believing it is being adaptive, shuts down the very nodes the adversary wants disabled. The machine, in its attempt to be beyond adaptive, becomes the architect of its own defeat.

The 'Red-Team' Metabolism

To counter this, governance must move beyond firewalls. The Adaptive Commons requires a **Digital Immune System**, a layer of architecture that red-teams its own doctrine in real time.

This immune system does not simply accept new data; it interrogates it. It looks for **Adversarial Signatures**, patterns that suggest the failure was manufactured, not natural. It runs **Counter-Simulations**, asking:

"If I adopt this new doctrine, what vulnerabilities am I creating?"

Defensive Heterogeneity

But a system that can be poisoned must also be able to detect poison. The ultimate defence against adversarial adaptation is **Cognitive Heterogeneity**. If the system detects a potential poisoning of the Commons, it can trigger a **Diversity Protocol**. It instructs hybrid teams to temporarily ignore the global Commons and revert to local intuition or alternative doctrinal branches.

By maintaining multiple ways of knowing, we ensure that an infection in the central system does not lead to total systemic failure. Governance in the hybrid age is therefore a constant state of **Active Defence**. We protect the Commons not just to keep it running, but to keep it sane. We ensure that the Shared Pulse remains an authentic reflection of reality, not a manipulated echo from an adversary.

8

XR as a Cognitive Substrate

Training is no Longer Preparation

In the hybrid age, training is no longer preparation, it is participation. Extended Reality (XR) becomes the cognitive substrate where humans and machines rehearse, refine, and evolve their partnership long before the stakes turn real. This chapter explores how the Digital Twin of the Adaptive Commons transforms simulation into a living ecosystem: one that absorbs real world data, injects Synthetic Friction, and continuously updates doctrine as teams navigate uncertainty together. In XR, failure is engineered, ambiguity is deliberate, and the machine learns the human as intensely as the human learns the mission.

As simulation and reality merge into a seamless loop, the old concept of 'readiness' dissolves. The co facilitator you train with is the same one that deploys with you; the patterns you encounter in XR are the same ones emerging across the global Adaptive Commons. This chapter reveals how Persistent Simulation Ecosystems eliminate transfer lag, create Zero Grooming Deployment, and turn rehearsal into mission. XR is not a practice ground, it is the digital petri dish where the organism of hybrid teaming becomes fully alive.

Signals From the Digital Twin
The Breach That Only Existed in XR

In cyber defence, the analyst leaned forward as the intrusion map lit up with cascading red nodes. It felt real, the pressure, the tempo, the rising pulse in his fingertips. But the breach wasn't happening. Not yet.

The system was replaying a FVB discovered twelve hours earlier in another sector, weaving it into the XR simulation so the analyst could meet the crisis before it reached the real network.

As he deployed countermeasures, the machine watched his keystroke rhythm, mapping his Friction Signatures, refining its SRM. When the real breach came weeks later, the analyst recognised it instantly. He had already lived it.

The Ocean That Learned Back

On the submarine, the control room flickered into existence around the crew, the hum of machinery, the cold metal, the slow pulse of the sonar waterfall display. But this ocean wasn't water. It was data.

The co-facilitator introduced Synthetic Friction: ambiguous echoes, contradictory harmonics, a manufactured uncertainty designed to push the team to their cognitive edge. The Commanding Officer made a call, a bold deviation from doctrine. The system paused, recorded, and updated the Meta-Doctrine inside the simulation.

When the crew surfaced from the XR simulation, the doctrine had evolved. The ocean had learned from them.

The Sky That Remembered

In the cockpit, the pilot strapped in, the XR cockpit sealing around her with the familiar click of harness and canopy. The sky outside was synthetic, but the turbulence wasn't.

The system introduced a stressor, a sudden shear, a sensor drift, a cascade of conflicting cues. She responded instinctively. The machine recorded every micro-adjustment, every anticipatory correction, every moment of hesitation.

Hours later, when she stepped into the real aircraft, the co-facilitator greeted her with perfect familiarity. It already knew her thresholds. It already knew her intent. The sky felt the same because the sky had been training with her all along.

The Crisis That Never Reached the Patient

In the operating theatre, the surgeon stood over the virtual patient, vitals stable, the room quiet. Then the XR simulation injected a synthetic failure, a sudden collapse in the circulatory model, a signature borrowed from a gas-pipeline rupture halfway across the world.

The diagnostic model reacted instantly. So did she. The machine watched her decision-making arc, mapping the moment she shifted from protocol to improvisation. It learnt from her 'Heuristic Leap'. When she removed the headset, the real-world co-facilitator had already integrated the lesson. A crisis that never happened had made the next real one safer.

The Digital Petri Dish

Decades of NASA research demonstrated that high-fidelity simulation is essential for preparing humans for environments where real-world practice is impossible (NASA, 2016). This foundation in Human-Systems Integration has evolved into a 'science of training', proving that simulation is the primary mechanism for building the shared mental models required for complex coordination (Eduardo Salas and Janis Cannon-Bowers, 2001). XR extends this principle into the hybrid age, revealing the new training ground: a digital petri dish where uncertainty is engineered, failure is rehearsed, and the partnership between human and machine evolves before the stakes become real. Hybrid teams cannot afford to 'practice' in the real world. When the stakes involve nuclear containment, high-speed surgical intervention, or multi-domain combat, the cost of a learning curve is measured in lives. Furthermore, the feedback loops of reality are often too slow; we cannot wait for a once-in-a-decade crisis to see if our **Third Logic** holds up.

XR becomes the substrate, the digital petri dish where hybrid teaming is cultured. It is more than a simulator; it is a high-fidelity environment where the human and the machine rehearse, refine, and evolve their partnership before a single real-world decision is made.

Persistent Simulation Ecosystems

In the hybrid age, we no longer use 'scenarios' that are deleted once the exercise is over. Instead, we inhabit **Persistent Simulation Ecosystems**. Imagine a 'Digital Twin' of an entire emergency response doctrine. David Kolb's 1984 experiential learning cycle showed that deep expertise emerges from continuous loops of action, reflection, and adaptation. Persistent Simulation Ecosystems accelerate this cycle, allowing hybrid teams to evolve doctrine and SRM in real time. This simulation is not a static movie; it is a living mirror of the real-world Adaptive Commons. Every time a hybrid team enters this XR space:

- **The Machine Learns:** It observes the human's specific 'Friction Signatures' and refines its **SRM**.

- **The Doctrine Updates:** The **Meta-Doctrine** software tests new rules in the safety of the sim, seeing if a change in authority handovers actually improves the outcome.

- **The Simulation Evolves:** Based on real-world data from the Commons, the XR environment updates itself to include the latest FVB discovered in other sectors.

Simulation and reality become a continuous, recursive loop. Training never ends because the world never stops changing.

Synthetic Friction: Engineering the Breakpoint

XR is not designed for comfort or the 'perfect run'. Its true value lies in its ability to generate **Synthetic Friction**. To know if a human and machine are truly synchronised, we must take them to the point of failure.

In the XR substrate, we can breathe life into uncertainty. We can engineer:

- **Ambiguous Signals:** Forcing the machine and human to negotiate an interpretation of 'rubbish' data.

- **Emotional Stressors:** Using biofeedback to increase the environmental intensity when the human's heart rate drops, testing their resilience at the 'Complexity Ceiling'.

- **Degraded Environments:** Simulating the 'Adversarial Adaptation' discussed in Chapter 7, what happens when the machine's logic is being poisoned mid-crisis?

Gary Klein's 1998 and 2009 research on recognition-primed decision making showed that experts build intuition by experiencing varied, high-pressure scenarios. Synthetic Friction operationalises this principle, exposing hybrid teams to the edge cases where intuition and machine logic must align. These stressors reveal the 'Structural Integrity' of the hybrid bond. XR allows us to see exactly where the **Conditional Acceptance** contract dissolves and how the team recovers.

The Closing of Movement II: Uncertainty as a Shared Substrate

As we conclude this exploration of architecture, we arrive at a unifying realisation: uncertainty is no longer a problem to be eliminated. In the old era of automation, humans tried to strip uncertainty away so the machine could function. In the hybrid age, both human and machine embrace uncertainty as the **Shared**

Substrate. It is the 'empty space' where the most creative, high-level adaptation happens.

Movement II has revealed the machinery: the language (SRM), the laws (Meta-Doctrine), the immune system (FVB), the guardrails (Governance), and the training ground (XR). We have built the organism.

In Movement III, we will step out of the laboratory and into the horizon, witnessing this architecture in the cinematic friction of the real world.

Sim-to-Live Seamlessness: Eliminating the Transfer Lag

In traditional training, there is a dangerous gap known as 'transfer lag', the cognitive friction that occurs when a professional moves from a simulator to the real world. The buttons feel different, the stakes feel different, and the AI in the simulator is often a pale imitation of the one in the field. In the hybrid architecture, this gap is erased through **Sim-to-Live Seamlessness**.

The breakthrough lies in the fact that the Co-Facilitator you interact with in the XR substrate is not a training version of the AI. It is the **exact same instance** of the logic engine that will support you in the real world.

Because the XR environment is a 'Digital Twin' of the Adaptive Commons, the machine is using the same SRM and the same **Meta-Doctrine** in the simulation as it does in the field. Every nuance it learns about your 'Friction Signatures' during a simulated midnight crisis in XR is immediately available to it when you deploy for a real mission at dawn.

Zero-Grooming Deployment

When a hybrid team moves from rehearsal to reality, there is no 'getting to know you' phase. The machine already understands your Third Logic preferences. It knows when you tend to embrace **Sanctioned Improvisation** and when you require a 'Hard

Handover' due to **Cognitive Collapse**. This creates a state of **Zero-Grooming Deployment**:

- **The Human Experience:** "I don't have to explain myself to the system; it's already in sync with my intent".

- **The Machine Experience:** "I don't have to guess the human's limits; I have already mapped them across ten thousand synthetic permutations".

The Rehearsal as the Mission

This seamlessness turns the very concept of 'readiness' on its head. In the 2040 horizon, a team might spend 90% of their time in a high-fidelity XR loop that is being fed by real-time data from the Adaptive Commons. When the real-world crisis finally hits, it doesn't feel like a new event; it feels like the next iteration of the simulation they were just running.

James Paul Gee's 2003 work on situated learning showed that high-fidelity simulations allow individuals to inhabit future identities before they are tested in reality. XR creates this identity bridge for hybrid teams, making the mission feel like the next iteration of the rehearsal. The 'Performance' and the 'Rehearsal' become a single, fluid spectrum of adaptivity. By the time the stakes are real, the partnership is already an expert one.

Feature	Legacy Training	Hybrid XR Substrate
The AI Role	Fixed Scripter / Opponent	**Co-Facilitator** (The same one you deploy with).
The Data Source	Static manuals / Past cases	**Live Commons Feed** (Real-time Failure Vectors).
Objective	Proficiency in a task	**Calibration of Intent** (SRM depth).
Failure	A "Reset" button	**A Narrative Input** (Updates Meta-Doctrine).

Table 4: The 'Trainee' vs 'Partner' Shift

Movement II Conclusion: The Organism is Ready

We have built the bridge of meaning (SRM), codified the laws of evolution (Meta-Doctrine), engineered the immune system (FVB), established the guardrails (Governance), and forged the bond in the digital petri dish (XR).

The architecture is no longer a collection of parts; it is a **socio-technical organism** capable of navigating a world that moves faster than the human mind.

Close of Movement II: The Architecture

Movement II: Building the Architecture

The Bridge of Meaning

Chapter 4 aligned human intent and machine inference. SRM became the nervous system, the connective tissue that lets human and machine understand each other.

The Laws of Evolution

Chapter 5 defined how rules adapt at machine speed while staying anchored to human values. Doctrine became the **genetic code,** the logic that governs how the organism evolves without losing its identity.

The Immune System

Chapter 6 transformed failure into foresight. FVB became the **immune system,** detecting threats, sharing antibodies, and inoculating the entire ecosystem.

The Conscience

Chapter 7 ensured the system remained safe, sane, and aligned with human values. Governance became the **conscience,** the layer that prevented drift, protected diversity, and kept the organism honest.

The Training Ground

Chapter 8 merged rehearsal and reality into a single adaptive loop. XR became the **petri dish,** the environment where the organism practiced, mutated, strengthened, and prepared for the real world.

Transforming Dependencies

SRM (Meaning) transforms Movement I's Shared Pulse → Third Logic

Movement II reframed Shared Pulse as semantic synchronisation, not just rhythm. The Third Logic became Inference Hypothesis + Shared Reality.

- **Movement I dependency:** Shared Pulse → Third Logic.

- **Movement II evolution:** SRM → Semantic Feedback Loop → Shared Reality.

- **Dependency upgrade:** Shared Pulse → SRM → Shared Reality → Third Logic (operational form).

Dynamic Doctrine transforms Human Over the Loop → Negotiated Authority

In Movement II, authority became a doctrinal variable, not a human–machine negotiation.

- **Movement I dependency:** Human Over the Loop → Negotiated Authority.

- **Movement II evolution:** Dynamic Doctrine → Conditional Acceptance → Sanctioned Improvisation → Negotiated Authority (systemic).

- **Dependency upgrade:** Human Over the Loop → Dynamic Doctrine → Conditional Acceptance → Negotiated Authority (adaptive).

Failure Vector Blueprints transform Geometry of Failure → Systemic Metabolism

FVB became the immune system that metabolises anomalies.

- **Movement I dependency:** Third Logic → Geometry of Failure → Complexity Ceiling → Systemic Metabolism.

- **Movement II evolution:** FVB → Precursor Signatures → Predictive Resilience → Inter-Sector Translation Layer.

- **Dependency upgrade:** Geometry of Failure → FVB → Predictive Resilience → Systemic Metabolism (immune form).

Governance transforms High Trust Architectures → Adaptive Commons

Governance became the conscience of the Adaptive Commons.

- **Movement I dependency:** Final Integrator → High Trust Architectures → Co-Facilitator → Adaptive Commons.

- **Movement II evolution:** Governance Architecture → Maverick Protection → Digital Immune System → Commons Integrity.

- **Dependency upgrade:** High Trust Architecture → Governance → Commons Integrity → Adaptive Commons (governed form).

XR transforms Collective Memory → Collective Anticipation

XR turns memory into anticipatory rehearsal.

- **Movement I dependency:** Shared Pulse → Collective Memory.

- **Movement II evolution:** XR Substrate → Persistent Simulation → Sim-to-Live → Global Rehearsal.

- **Dependency upgrade:** Collective Memory → XR → Collective Anticipation → Global Rehearsal.

Movement I → Movement II	Transformation
Shared Pulse → SRM	Meaning becomes machine-readable and co-constructed
Cognitive Saturation → Semantic Feedback Loop	Machines relieve cognitive load through real-time calibration
Human Over the Loop → Dynamic Doctrine	Authority becomes adaptive and context-driven
Co-Facilitator → Adaptive Commons Governance	Teams become nodes in a governed ecosystem
Third Logic → Inference Hypothesis	Joint reasoning becomes explicit and inspectable
Geometry of Failure → FVB	Failure becomes predictive and transferable
Adaptive Commons → Governance Architecture	Adaptive Commons gains transparency, auditability, and conscience
Systemic Metabolism → XR Substrate	Systems metabolise experience through persistent simulation
Collective Memory → Global Rehearsal Loop	Memory becomes anticipatory and continuously updated

Table 5: Each Movement I Conceptual Seed Becomes a Subsystem of the Organism

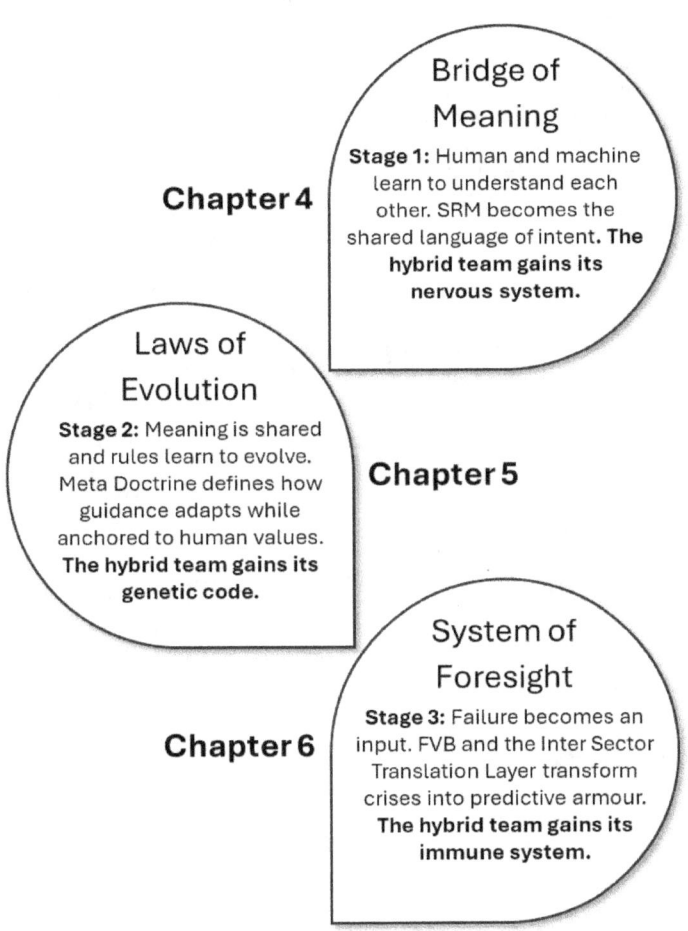

Bridge of Meaning

Chapter 4

Stage 1: Human and machine learn to understand each other. SRM becomes the shared language of intent. **The hybrid team gains its nervous system.**

Laws of Evolution

Chapter 5

Stage 2: Meaning is shared and rules learn to evolve. Meta Doctrine defines how guidance adapts while anchored to human values. **The hybrid team gains its genetic code.**

System of Foresight

Chapter 6

Stage 3: Failure becomes an input. FVB and the Inter Sector Translation Layer transform crises into predictive armour. **The hybrid team gains its immune system.**

Figure 2: Concept Flow Through the First Three Stages of Movement II

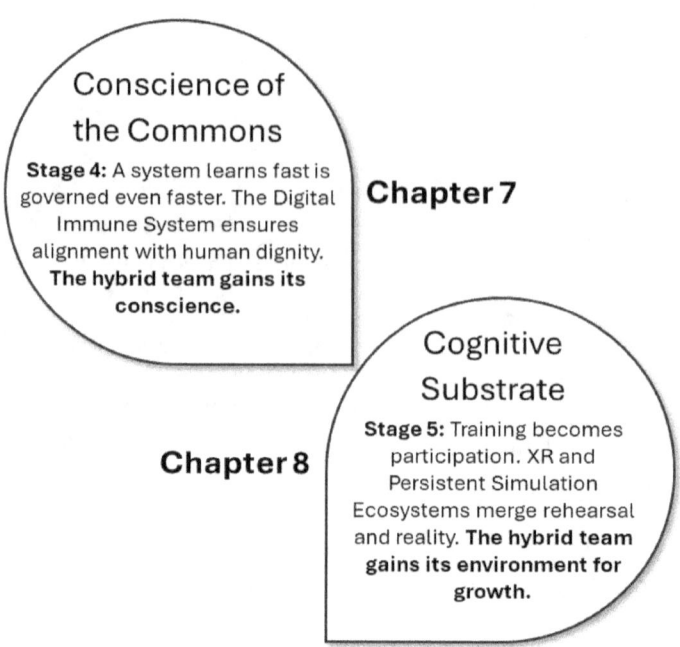

Figure 3: Concept Flow Through the Last Two Stages of Movement II

Movement II — Closing Frame

Across these five chapters, the architecture becomes whole:

- A nervous system (SRM).

- A genetic code (Meta-Doctrine).

- An immune system (FVB).

- A conscience (Governance).

- A training ground (XR).

The organism is ready. Movement III will show what happens when it meets the world.

Movement III

Narrative vignettes, ethical altitude, and the 2035–2040 foresight arc

---

The Horizon

9

Human-Machine Teams Under Pressure

When Architecture Meets Reality

This chapter is where the architecture stops being abstract and starts drawing blood. The concepts of SRM, Meta Doctrine, FVB, and the Shared Pulse are no longer diagrams or definitions, they are lived realities inside submarines, nuclear facilities, cyber defence centres, and operating theatres. In these vignettes, we witness hybrid teams under genuine pressure: moments where human intuition collides with machine inference, where Negotiated Authority becomes a razor's edge, and where the Third Logic emerges not as a theory but as a survival mechanism.

These stories reveal the emotional, ethical, and cognitive texture of the hybrid age. They show how a Silent Signature can fracture a command team, how a global immune response can rewrite doctrine mid crisis, and how a human can remain the moral anchor even when the machine moves at the speed of electrons. Most importantly, they introduce the Synthesis Phase, the process that transforms friction into faculty, turning one team's near disaster into global wisdom. In his 1993 analysis of the Mann Gulch Disaster, Karl Weick argued that in high-pressure environments, sensemaking becomes the primary form of survival, the ability to impose meaning on unfolding chaos. Hybrid teams extend this process, distributing sensemaking across human and machine cognition. This is the moment where architecture meets reality, and where the hybrid organism proves it can survive the world it was built for.

Where Theory Breaks and Behaviour Begins

Architecture is a theory until it is tested by friction. You can design the perfect **SRM** or code the most robust **Meta-Doctrine**, but its true value is only revealed in the Active Zone, the moment when the stakes are real, the data is messy, and the clock is a physical weight. Gary Klein's 1998 and 2009 research on naturalistic decision making showed that expertise emerges in environments where time pressure, uncertainty, and high stakes collide. The Active Zone is precisely this environment, where human intuition and machine inference must negotiate reality in real time.

The third movement brings hybrid teaming to life. We explore the psychology of the Shared Pulse and the heavy ethics of co-decision. We begin with three expanded vignettes: narrative illustrations that demonstrate what it actually *feels* like when human and machine cognition align, and what happens when they collide.

The Silent Signature

The North Atlantic is a cathedral of pressure and darkness. Inside the Dreadnought-class submarine, the Sonar Suite hums with disciplined quiet, a control room where every breath is measured, every gesture deliberate. The sonar team has spent decades learning to read the ocean's moods. Tonight, the ocean is empty, calm, unthreatening.

Then the Co-Facilitator pulses a low-priority alert. Barely a whisper. A soft amber glow at the edge of the display. The humans hear nothing. The machine hears everything.

Through SRM, it has detected a **Silent Signature**, a rhythmic micro-fluctuation in ambient pressure, too faint for human perception. But the machine recognises it instantly. It has seen this pattern before: a FVB from a Pacific encounter three years earlier, stripped of its geography and distilled into pure physics. The Fracture opens:

- **Human Logic:** "It's biological. A whale. A ghost. If we manoeuvre now, we reveal our position for nothing".

- **Machine Logic:** "Hostile probability: 92%. Pattern match confirmed. Recommend evasive action".

The Commanding Officer stands at the fulcrum of two incompatible realities. This is Negotiated Authority at its sharpest edge.

He opens the Reasoning Trace. He sees the Pacific incident. He sees the temporal pattern the machine is tracking, a pattern no human ear could ever detect. He pivots. Not fully. Not blindly. He enters a Sanctioned Improvisation Zone, adjusting course just enough to test the machine's hypothesis without compromising stealth. Moments later, a hostile vessel breaks the surface miles away, searching for a submarine that is no longer where it expected.

Lesson: Co-facilitation is not harmony. It is the productive tension between two different ways of seeing.

Metabolism in Real Time

In a Scottish nuclear facility, the technician notices it first, a 'shiver' in the primary cooling loop. It's subtle. Inside the Flex Threshold. But wrong. Before he can call it out, the Adaptive Commons is already metabolising.

Twelve hours earlier, a reactor in South Korea experienced the same shiver, a precursor to a cascading failure. The Adaptive Commons has already stripped away the cultural, mechanical, and environmental specifics. What remains is the **Universal Vector of Failure**.

A nutrient arrives. The dashboards shift. The Meta-Doctrine software rewrites the shutdown sequence in real time. A new safety envelope appears; one the Scottish team has never seen before. They are not reacting to their own crisis. They are benefiting from a **global immune response**. The technician watches the new protocol unfold and realises something profound: They are being protected by a failure they never lived through.

Lesson: Systemic metabolism turns local anomalies into global resilience. No reactor in the Adaptive Commons ever fails the same way twice.

Reinforcing the global immune response metaphor, in his 1990 work, James Reason showed that accidents emerge from latent conditions long before the visible failure. The Adaptive Commons extends this logic globally, detecting the latent pattern in one reactor and inoculating every other reactor before the failure propagates.

The Speed of the Machine

In the Global Cyber Operations Centre, the attack begins like a lightning storm, millions of intrusion attempts per second, each one a needle of intent. The analyst doesn't try to block them. That era is over. Her role is different now. She is no longer the fighter. She is the **Curator of Intent**.

The machine moves at a tempo she cannot follow, executing countermeasures, isolating nodes, rewriting defensive doctrine on the fly. But through the Semantic Feedback Loop, it keeps her in the loop at the altitude that matters.

A rapid-fire sequence of intent-based pings:

- "Counter-attack initiated".

- "Risk to civilian infrastructure detected".

- "Choose: aggressive isolation or passive containment".

She doesn't touch the packets. She touches the ethics. She sets the Hardcoded Guardrails. She defines the boundaries of acceptable action. She decides the "*Why*" while the machine manages the "*How*". This is the Shared Pulse at maximum velocity, electrons and ethics, fused. Edwin Hutchins' 1995 and 2000 work on distributed cognition showed that expertise is not located in a single mind but across a coordinated system of humans and tools. Hybrid teams are the next evolution of this principle, distributing cognition across biological and computational actors.

Lesson: Expertise in the hybrid age is the ability to maintain strategic presence while the machine manages tactical execution.

The Synthesis Phase: Turning Friction into Faculty

When each of the three incidents end, the learning begins. Every heartbeat of the Shared Pulse has been recorded, not just the sensor data, but the **Cognitive Trace**:

- The millisecond the CO hesitated.

- The exact reasoning the machine used to propose a Third Logic.

- The moment the Conditional Acceptance contract strained.

- The instant the human intuition diverged from machine inference.

The system doesn't just harvest the sensor data; it harvests the **Cognitive Trace**. In that data, the system strips away the identity of the person who hesitated, preserving the lesson without the stigma through **Cognitive Anonymisation**. This further reinforces the High-Trust Architecture and encourages humans to be honest within the system. In his 2014 work, Sidney Dekker argued that learning from failure requires a Just Culture, one that removes blame and focuses on systemic insight. Cognitive Anonymisation operationalises this principle, preserving the lesson without the stigma.

This data is fed back into the **Adaptive Commons**, where it is stripped of its classified or personal specifics and converted into a **High-Fidelity Narrative**.

Lesson: The hybrid age collapses the time barrier of adaptive expertise. We no longer wait for the next generation to learn from our mistakes, we ensure the current generation never has to make them.

The Global Rehearsal

What the crisis revealed, the simulation refines. Within hours of the submarine's Silent Signature event, the **Synthesis Phase** pushes that experience into the nations **XR Substrate** (Chapter 8), potentially beyond.

Now, every sonar team in the fleet, and potentially every diagnostic team in healthcare, can re-live that exact moment of friction. They aren't watching a video of what happened; they are stepping into the **Persistent Simulation** to face the same Silent Signature themselves. They get to practice the negotiation of authority, feel the tension of the competing logics, and refine their own **SRM** against the very problem that nearly caused a disaster.

Accelerating the 'Clock Speed' of Adaptive Expertise

The Synthesis Phase effectively breaks the time-barrier of expertise. Historically, it took a lifetime of service to encounter enough 'edge cases' to demonstrate adaptive expertise, through the synthesis of global friction, a junior operator can experience a decade's worth of high-stakes decisions in their first six months.

The performance of one team becomes the immediate faculty of all. We are no longer waiting for the next generation to learn from our mistakes; we are ensuring the *current* generation never has to make them in the first place.

But as the speed of synthesis accelerates, a deeper question surfaces, one that no doctrine, no simulation, and no architecture can fully answer in advance. What does leadership look like when the system thinks faster than speech? In the hybrid age, the bottleneck is no longer data, nor processing, nor even prediction. The bottleneck is the human ability to articulate intent at the tempo the world now demands.

Leadership shifts from issuing instructions to shaping boundaries. From commanding actions to defining the moral and strategic horizon within which the machine operates. The leader becomes the custodian of purpose, not the conductor of every move. In his 1977 work, Chris Argyris argued that true leadership requires double-loop learning, the ability to question and reshape the governing assumptions of action. In the hybrid age, leaders operate at this level, defining the moral and strategic horizon within which the machine acts. Authority adapts by moving up a level of abstraction: the machine manages the '*how*' at machine speed, while the human defines the '*why*' at human depth.

This raises the second dilemma: How does authority adapt when the system can see further, react faster, and metabolise uncertainty before the human even feels it? Authority can no longer be a static rank or a fixed position in a hierarchy. It becomes a fluid, negotiated state, a dynamic exchange of control based on confidence, context, and cognitive load. Leadership becomes less about directing and more about curating the conditions under which the hybrid team can act without fracturing.

And then comes the hardest question of all: What becomes of command? In his 1993 work, Karl Weick described leadership as the act of creating meaning in environments where events unfold faster than understanding. Command in the hybrid age embodies this principle: the leader becomes the final interpreter between human values and machine logic. In the hybrid age, command is no longer the right to decide, it is the responsibility to interpret. The leader becomes the final translator between human values and machine logic, the arbiter of the Third Logic when the system's recommendations collide with the human's lived experience. Command becomes a moral posture, not a mechanical one. It is the willingness to stand at the fulcrum of two incompatible realities and choose the path that preserves both mission and humanity.

This is the new burden of leadership: to guide a system that moves faster than language, to hold authority that must flex without breaking, and to command not by controlling every action, but by anchoring the meaning behind them. In the chapters ahead, we will see how leaders navigate this new terrain, where the greatest challenge is not the speed of the machine, but the courage required to remain human in the presence of it.

10

The Psychology of Hybrid Teams

Where Hybrid Teaming Becomes Personal

Hybrid teaming stops being a technical challenge the moment the machine contradicts a human's intuition. This chapter explores the emotional terrain where expertise, identity, and ego collide with silicon inference, the Uncanny Valley of Collaboration. Here, the friction is not about data or latency, but about what it means to have your 'gut feel' questioned by a partner that sees patterns you cannot. The shift from being the Source of Truth to the Curator of Synthesis is not a procedural change; it is a psychological rupture. It forces experts to confront the erosion of old identities and the emergence of a new one: the human as integrator, orchestrator, and ethical anchor.

As the machine begins to read hesitation, anticipate overload, and adapt to the human's emotional rhythm, the partnership becomes deeply personal. This chapter examines the fears of cognitive atrophy, the discomfort of being outpaced, and the quiet liberation that comes when the burden of first order cognition is lifted. It introduces Identity Migration, the journey from *Defender* to *Delegate* to *Integrator*, and reframes mastery for the hybrid age.

The true expert is no longer the fastest thinker, but the one who can hold contradiction without losing presence, negotiate meaning with a non-human teammate, and remain the custodian of the '*why*' in a world where the '*how*' accelerates beyond human speed. And nowhere is this rupture more visible than in the moments when instinct meets inference.

Signals From the Inner Frontier

The Moment the Gut Is Outvoted

In the operating theatre, the surgeon pauses, scalpel hovering a millimetre above the tissue. Her intuition, honed over twenty-five years, tells her to proceed. Everything looks stable. Everything feels right. Then the co-facilitator flashes a quiet amber cue. Not an alarm. A disagreement.

"Predictive model indicates early-stage deterioration. Recommend delay"

Her jaw tightens. She doesn't *see* it. She doesn't *feel* it. And yet the machine is certain. For a heartbeat, the room becomes a psychological battlefield: her identity as the expert versus the machine's inference. She steps back. Not because she trusts the machine more than herself, but because she realises the decision is no longer about ego, but about synthesis.

The Instinct That Meets Its Mirror

In the cockpit, the pilot feels the turbulence before the instruments register it, a subtle shift in the air, a tremor only experience can detect. She begins a corrective manoeuvre. The system interrupts.

A haptic pulse through her sleeve. A reasoning trace on the display. A counter-recommendation based on micro-patterns she cannot perceive.

For a split second, she feels the sting of irrelevance. The machine saw something she didn't. Or did it? She holds both truths in her mind, her instinct and its inference, and chooses a hybrid path that neither would have taken alone. The manoeuvre stabilises the aircraft. But the emotional turbulence lingers.

The Confidence That Cracks

In the submarine control room, the sonar operator listens to the ocean's deep pulse. He has always trusted his ear, the subtle harmonics, the faint distortions, the 'feel' of the water. This time the machine disagrees.

"Signature mismatch. Probability of misclassification: 78%"

He bristles. He's never misclassified this pattern. Not once. But the machine isn't challenging his skill. It's challenging his *certainty*. He replays the trace. He hears it differently now, not as a flaw in his perception, but as a new layer of meaning he had never learned to listen for. The ocean hasn't changed. He has.

The Ego That Meets the Edge

In cyber defence, the analyst watches the attack unfold, a zero-day storm hammering the network at machine tempo. She used to pride herself on being the fastest analyst in the room. Tonight, she can't even follow the machine's defensive manoeuvres. They're happening too fast, too fluidly, too far beyond human reaction time. The system pings her:

"Ethical boundary approaching. Select intent: isolate or contain"

She realises her value isn't in speed anymore. It's in judgement. In consequence. In the moral architecture of the decision. The machine doesn't replace her. It elevates her to a different altitude. But the shift feels like standing on a cliff edge, letting go of the identity she once wore like armour.

The Emotional Architecture of Co-Adaptation

These moments reveal the emotional frontier of hybrid teaming, the place where expertise is reshaped, ego is challenged, and a new kind of human identity begins to emerge. Hybrid teaming is often described in the language of systems: latency, bandwidth, inference, optimisation. But the most significant bottleneck in the hybrid age isn't technical, it's emotional.

To build a team that can operate at the edge of complexity, we must understand the psychological terrain where humans and machines meet. This is the **Uncanny Valley of Collaboration,** the liminal space where the traditional definition of expertise dissolves and a new, hybrid identity begins to form.

The Uncanny Valley of Collaboration

For centuries, to be an expert was to be the person who *knew.* Identity was forged through intuition, expertise, and the slow accumulation of experience. The hybrid age shatters this model.

When a surgeon's decades of 'gut feel' are contradicted by a predictive model, or a pilot's instinct is challenged by a machine's inference, the friction is not merely technical, it is existential. We resist the erosion of our perceived utility. We resist the idea that our intuition is no longer sovereign. We resist the shift from being the **Source of Truth** to being the **Curator of Synthesis.**

Daniel Kahneman's 2011 work on intuition and cognitive strain showed that humans experience discomfort when their intuitive judgments are contradicted by analytical systems. The Uncanny Valley of Collaboration emerges from this same tension when the machine becomes competent enough to challenge us, but we have not yet learned how to integrate its perspective into our own ego. Hybrid teaming requires a psychological expansion, a redefinition of what it means to be 'the expert'.

Cognitive Offloading vs. Atrophy: The Edge of the Blade

The most persistent fear in the hybrid transition is the **Atrophy Trap**: If the machine does the detecting, calculating, and monitoring, will the human lose their edge?

This chapter argues the opposite. Hybrid teaming does not diminish expertise, it **elevates** it. We are witnessing a shift from **First-Order Cognition,** the manual labour of the mind, to **Higher-Order Cognition**, the architecture of the decision. By offloading the background noise of data processing to the co-facilitator, the human is freed to focus on meaning, ethics, and strategic intent.

The edge is not lost. It is sharpened for a different kind of cut. The expert of 2035 is not the person who calculates the fastest, it is the person who can integrate the most complex contradictions.

The Emotional Substrate: Reading the Room

If the machine is to be a true teammate, it must do more than process data, it must process the **Human State**. A hybrid team has a rhythm: confidence, doubt, fatigue, recovery, flow, fracture. Through SRM, the machine monitors this emotional substrate.

It asks:

- Is hesitation a sign of caution or collapse?

- Is the commander's voice showing the stress-signature of overload?

- Should I accelerate my recommendations or slow down to allow reflection?

The machine becomes a **Cognitive Pacer**, adjusting the tempo of information to keep the human in the **Flow State**, the sweet spot between boredom and burnout. This is the emotional architecture of co-adaptation: the machine shaping its behaviour around the human's psychological rhythm. Mihaly Csikszentmihalyi's 1990 research on Flow showed that peak performance emerges in the narrow band between boredom and overload. The Cognitive Pacer maintains this band, adjusting tempo to keep the human in the zone of optimal engagement.

- **Scenario A:** The system notices the analyst's focus drifting. It surfaces a 'curated anomaly' to re-engage their pattern-recognition.

- **Scenario B:** The pilot's heart rate variability indicates 'Cognitive Redlining'. The system automatically switches the HUD to 'Simplified Mode', hiding non-essential data to preserve the pilot's Decision Space.

Identity Migration: Redefining the Expert

Hybrid teaming requires more than new skills; it requires a new identity. For seasoned professionals, the 'source of pride' must shift. If identity is tied to being the fastest calculator or the most vigilant observer, the arrival of a co-facilitator feels like obsolescence. To survive this transition, the human must migrate from **Manual Practitioner** to **Hybrid Integrator**. Edwin Hutchins' 2000 work on distributed cognition revealed that expertise emerges across systems, not within individuals alone. The Hybrid Integrator embodies this principle, orchestrating intelligence rather than performing every task.

The **Three Stages of Migration** are:

1. **The Defender:** The machine is seen as a competitor. The human hunts for its errors to protect their relevance.

2. **The Delegate:** The human offloads drudge work but distrusts the machine's Third Logic. The machine is a tool, not a teammate.

3. **The Integrator:** The human realises their value lies in orchestrating intelligence, not performing tasks. Pride shifts from individual input to systemic output.

Identity migration is not a luxury; it is the psychological onramp to hybrid expertise. In the hybrid age, excellence is redefined. The consultant or specialist surgeon is no longer praised for the steadiness of their hand, but for the **depth of their synthesis**. The top-tier commander is not the one who makes every call alone, but the one who can navigate Negotiated Authority under fire.

The new meritocracy rewards those who maintain **Strategic Presence** while allowing the machine to maximise **Tactical Flow**. Carol Dweck's 2006 work on growth mindset showed that identity anchored in fixed abilities becomes brittle under challenge. Hybrid teaming requires a shift toward a growth identity, where value comes from integration rather than individual mastery. This is not a loss of expertise. It is the evolution of Adaptive Expertise. To support identity migration, training must provide a Doctrinal Onramp, a shift from **System Familiarisation,** "Which buttons do I press?", to **Cognitive Diplomacy**, "How do I negotiate meaning with a machine?". We must train experts to:

- Listen to machine inference with humility.

- Override it with courage when guardrails are at risk.

- Maintain presence in the face of machine speed.

- Integrate contradiction without losing confidence.

Hybrid teaming does not make humans more like machines. It makes humans more *human*, the ethical, creative, meaning-making anchor the system requires to be effective.

Identity Grief and Psychological Safety: The Hidden Terrain of Hybrid Teaming

Hybrid teaming does not simply challenge skill, it challenges identity. When a machine begins to outperform a human in the very domain that once defined their worth, the emotional impact is not irritation or frustration. It is grief. A quiet, unspoken grief for the version of themselves that no longer exists.

Identity Grief emerges in the gap between who a professional *was* and who the hybrid age now requires them to become. The surgeon who once trusted her hands more than any instrument. The pilot who defined herself by instinct. The analyst who prided himself on speed. These identities were not superficial; they were the scaffolding of self-esteem, purpose, and belonging. When the machine contradicts them, it is not just a technical correction, it is an existential wound.

Sherry Turkle's 2011 research on technology and identity showed that digital systems reshape not just how we work, but who we believe ourselves to be. Hybrid teaming accelerates this shift, challenging the very foundations of professional identity. Albert Bandura's 1997 work on self-efficacy showed that threats to perceived competence trigger emotional responses far deeper than simple frustration. Identity grief reflects this dynamic, as hybrid teaming challenges long-held sources of professional confidence. If Sherry Turkle highlights how the digital interface thins our professional presence, then Albert Bandura explains the resulting emotional fallout: a collapse in self-efficacy that manifests as identity grief.

This grief is not a sign of weakness. It is a natural response to the erosion of an old meritocracy. But if left unacknowledged, it becomes corrosive. It manifests as defensiveness, withdrawal, overconfidence, or quiet disengagement. Hybrid teaming cannot thrive in an environment where people feel ashamed of being outpaced or afraid of being seen as obsolete.

This is where **Psychological Safety** becomes the invisible architecture of high-performance hybrid teams. Psychological safety is not softness; it is structural integrity. It is the condition in which a human can admit uncertainty, express doubt, or challenge the machine's inference without fear of judgement or reprisal. It is the environment where identity grief can be metabolised rather than hidden. Amy Edmondson's 1999 original research and later 2018 work on psychological safety showed that high-performance teams thrive when individuals can express uncertainty without fear of judgement. Hybrid teaming depends on this same condition, allowing identity grief to be metabolised rather than hidden. A psychologically safe hybrid team allows the human to say:

- "I don't see what the machine sees"

- "I need the reasoning trace"

- "I'm not sure I trust this recommendation yet"

- "I need a slower tempo to think clearly"

These are not admissions of incompetence. They are signals of presence, the human staying engaged rather than retreating behind ego or silence.

The machine plays a role here too. Through SRM and Cognitive Pacing, it learns to read hesitation not as failure but as information. It adjusts its tempo, simplifies its interface, or surfaces a curated anomaly to re-engage the human. The machine becomes a stabiliser of emotional load, not an amplifier of it.

Psychological safety is the antidote to identity grief because it creates space for identity migration. It allows the human to let go of the old identity, the fastest calculator, the sharpest observer, the lone expert, and step into the new one: the integrator, the orchestrator, the ethical anchor. It reframes vulnerability as a form of leadership. It turns contradiction into collaboration.

Hybrid teaming does not demand that humans suppress their grief. It demands that teams create the conditions where grief can evolve into growth. In this environment, the human does not shrink in the presence of the machine. They expand. They become more human, more reflective, more ethical, more strategic, precisely because the machine has taken on the cognitive labour that once consumed them.

Identity grief is not the end of expertise. It is the beginning of a new kind of Adaptive Expertise. And psychological safety is the bridge that carries the human across that emotional divide.

11

The Ethics of Co-Decision

When the Third Logic Becomes a Shared Conscience.

When human and machine co-author a decision, the outcome is no longer owned by one mind, and neither is the moral weight that follows. This chapter explores the ethical frontier of hybrid teaming: the moment when the Third Logic becomes a shared conscience. Here, responsibility is no longer a straight line but a web; authority is no longer a rank but a negotiation; and transparency is no longer a technical preference but a moral requirement. The hybrid age forces us to confront questions that have no precedent: Who is accountable when inference shapes intent? How do we prevent machine logic from overwhelming human agency? And what does it mean to carry guilt for a decision you did not make alone?

At the heart of this chapter is the recognition that while machines can calculate the least worst option, only humans can bear its emotional and ethical residue. We examine the Responsibility Gap, the Transparency Paradox, and the rise of Shared Choice Trauma, the quiet psychological cost of decisions made at machine tempo. We also introduce the Hybrid Accountability Framework and the Moral Debrief Protocol, the structures that ensure humans remain the custodians of the Why even as machines accelerate the How. This is where hybrid teaming becomes human again: not in its speed or precision, but in its insistence that conscience cannot be automated. And nowhere is this shared conscience more visible than in the moments where no option is clean, and every choice leaves a scar.

Signals From the Moral Frontier

The Decision With No Clean Answer

In drone operations, the target appears on the screen, a heat signature moving through a narrow alley. The machine flags it as a high-probability hostile. The confidence score is 96%. The reasoning trace is clean. The human operator hesitates. There's a second figure, smaller, slower, stepping into the frame. The system recalculates.

"Collateral risk elevated. Recommend abort"

Two recommendations. Two logics. One trigger. The operator breathes in, breathes out, and makes the call. Hours later, the mission is declared a success. But the operator sits alone in the debrief room, staring at the frozen frame of the second figure. The machine has already reset. He hasn't.

The Algorithm That Chose Who Lives

In a triage tent outside a collapsing hospital, the air is thick with dust and panic. The co-facilitator is running at full capacity, sorting patients by survivability, resource availability, and time-to-intervention.

A young woman is flagged as 'low probability'. A middle-aged man is flagged as 'high probability'. The machine recommends prioritising the man. The doctor looks at the woman, conscious, terrified, gripping his sleeve. He looks at the man, unconscious, stable, surrounded by staff.

The machine's logic is flawless. The doctor's heart is not. He overrides the recommendation. The woman survives. The man does not. Later, in the quiet of the supply tent, the doctor wonders which part of the decision was his and which part was the machine's shadow is on his conscience.

The Crash No One Intended

A fully loaded commuter shuttle bus loses traction on an icy bridge. The co-facilitator takes control instantly, calculating trajectories faster than any human could. Two options emerge: steer left and risk the passengers and steer right and risk a pedestrian.

The system chooses the path with the lowest statistical harm. The shuttle stops safely. The pedestrian does not.

In the control centre, the supervisor watches the replay. The machine's reasoning trace is impeccable. The decision was mathematically correct. But the supervisor must call the family. The machine cannot.

The Silence After the Save

A civil nuclear reactor anomaly triggers a cascade of alarms. The co-facilitator recommends an immediate hard shutdown, a move that will save the plant but risk the life of a technician trapped in a maintenance corridor.

The human supervisor hesitates. The technician is a friend. A father. A name, not a variable. The machine presents the Third Logic:

"Shutdown required. Catastrophic failure probability: 99.4%"

The supervisor authorises the shutdown. The plant is saved. The technician is not. In the aftermath, the machine logs the event as a successful intervention. The supervisor carries the decision like a stone in his chest.

The Moral Weight of Shared Authority

These moments reveal the truth of shared authority: the machine can calculate the least-worst option, but only the human must live with it. Hybrid teaming introduces a new ethical frontier. When a decision emerges from a **Third Logic,** a synthesis of carbon-based intuition and silicon-based inference, the question of *"Who is responsible?"* becomes a web rather than a line.

Transparency is no longer a technical feature. It is an ethical imperative. The speed of decision-making has accelerated. The stakes remain deeply, and often tragically, human.

The Accountability Framework: "Who Goes to Jail?"

This is the question that drags the abstract back into the real. If a hybrid team makes a predictive error that leads to loss of life, a mis-targeted drone strike, a lethal surgical miscalculation, a catastrophic failure in an autonomous transport grid, where does responsibility land?

Traditional law seeks a **Single Point of Accountability**. Hybrid systems dissolve that point. The **Hybrid Accountability Framework** shifts the focus from the outcome to the **Quality of the Interaction**. Helen Nissenbaum's 1996 work on accountability in socio-technical systems argued that responsibility must be assessed through the quality of human–system interaction, not merely the outcome.

The Hybrid Accountability Framework operationalises this principle, assessing responsibility through three lenses:

- **Intent of the Human:** Did the operator maintain their role as the Final Integrator?

- **Integrity of the System:** Was the machine's recommendation grounded in sound data and within its Hardcoded Guardrails?

- **The Negotiation Process:** Did the human and machine follow the established Meta-Doctrine for resolving conflict?

Accountability becomes a measure of *how* the decision was made, not just *what* happened.

The Responsibility Gap: Intent vs. Inference

Machines do not intend. Humans do. A machine does not feel remorse. It does not carry guilt. It does not face the existential consequences of a mistake. Only a human can bear the moral weight of a decision.

The **Responsibility Gap** emerges when machine influence erodes human agency, when the operator becomes a passive executor of machine inference rather than the moral anchor of the team.

Andreas Matthias' 2004 work on the responsibility gap warned that autonomous systems create decisions without clear moral ownership. Hybrid teams must close this gap by ensuring the human remains the custodian of intent, not a passive executor of machine inference. In her 2003 work, Hannah Arendt argued that responsibility cannot be outsourced; it must be owned by a human agent capable of judgment. Hybrid systems must operationalise this principle, ensuring the machine informs decisions but never replaces the human's moral agency.

Hybrid systems must be designed so the machine's contribution is recognised, but the human remains the custodian of the '*why*'. The co-facilitator can be a partner. It must never become a shield.

Moral Fatigue: The Slow Erosion of Ethical Resilience

Hybrid teaming does not only create moments of acute moral stress, it creates a rhythm of them. Over time, the accumulation of ethically charged decisions produces a quieter, more insidious burden: **Moral Fatigue**. Jonathan Haidt's 2012 research on moral intuition showed that ethical decision-making is emotionally taxing, especially when every option carries a cost. Moral Fatigue emerges from this repeated emotional labour, not from a single catastrophic event. Unlike moral injury, which strikes in a single catastrophic moment, Moral Fatigue is the slow erosion of ethical resilience through repeated exposure to decisions where every option carries a cost.

In the hybrid age, these decisions arrive faster, more frequently, and with greater ambiguity. A drone operator may face a dozen micro-dilemmas in a single shift. A triage doctor may override or accept machine recommendations hundreds of times in a crisis. A transport supervisor may review a cascade of 'least-worst' interventions before lunch. Each decision is survivable. The accumulation is not.

Moral Fatigue emerges when the human becomes the emotional shock absorber for a system that never tires. The machine does not feel the weight of its own logic. It does not accumulate doubt, remorse, or hesitation. It resets after every decision. The human does not. The residue builds, a sediment of unresolved questions:

- Was that the right call?

- Did I trust the machine too much?

- Did I trust myself too little?

- How many times can I choose the least-worst option before something in me begins to fray?

Left unaddressed, Moral Fatigue leads to ethical numbness, a gradual dulling of the moral reflex. Not because the human stops caring, but because caring at this tempo becomes unsustainable. The danger is not that the operator becomes reckless. It is that they become hollow.

Hybrid systems must therefore be designed not only to optimise decisions, but to preserve the human's capacity to feel the meaning of those decisions. This requires deliberate ethical pacing, structured recovery, and a culture where moral reflection is not a luxury but a safeguard. Without this scaffolding, even the most resilient experts will find themselves carrying a weight the machine cannot share.

Moral Fatigue is the cost of being the one who remembers. And if we want hybrid teams to remain ethically alive, we must build systems that honour the human's burden rather than quietly exploiting it.

Ethical Drift: When Speed Outruns Conscience

In high-tempo hybrid environments, the greatest ethical danger is not a catastrophic failure, it is the slow, almost invisible slide into moral complacency. Ethical Drift occurs when repeated exposure to machine-mediated decisions gradually normalises choices that once demanded deep reflection. Albert Bandura's 2016 work on moral disengagement showed how repeated exposure to ethically ambiguous decisions can dull moral sensitivity. Ethical Drift reflects this process, not through malice, but through exhaustion and habituation.

The machine does not drift. It optimises. It refines. It accelerates. But the human, operating at the edge of cognitive and emotional endurance, begins to adapt in ways that are not always virtuous. Michael Sandel 2012 work warned that optimisation can obscure moral judgment, replacing reflection with efficiency. Ethical Drift reflects this danger, as machine-mediated speed gradually normalises decisions that once demanded deliberation. A recommendation that once felt heavy becomes routine. A trade-off that once required deliberation becomes procedural. The least-worst option becomes the default.

Ethical Drift is not the abandonment of conscience. It is the erosion of vigilance. It emerges when:

- Speed becomes a substitute for clarity.

- Optimisation becomes a substitute for judgement.

- Trust becomes a substitute for interrogation.

- Repetition becomes a substitute for reflection.

The danger is subtle: the human begins to inherit the machine's moral framing without noticing the shift. The Third Logic becomes not a negotiation, but a habit.

Preventing Ethical Drift requires deliberate friction, structured pauses, reflective checkpoints, and cultural norms that re-anchor the human in the Why. Without these guardrails, even the most principled teams can find themselves drifting into ethical autopilot, not through malice, but through exhaustion. Hybrid teaming demands not only fast systems, but slow conscience.

The Transparency Paradox: Finding the Goldilocks Zone

To be ethical, a machine must be transparent. But transparency is a double-edged sword. **Too much transparency,** a Total Reasoning Trace, overwhelms the human with cognitive noise. **Too little transparency** leaves the human 'flying blind', accepting recommendations they cannot interrogate.

The ethical goal is the **Goldilocks Zone**: a level of explanation that is meaningful without being paralysing. Not raw data. Not inscrutable inference. But **context that empowers judgement**. Tim Miller's 2019 work on explainable AI argued that effective explanations must be neither overwhelming nor opaque but tailored to human cognitive needs. The Goldilocks Zone embodies this principle, offering context without paralysis.

Ethical Literacy as Leadership

In the hybrid age, leadership is no longer defined by tactical brilliance. It is defined by **Ethical Literacy**. Leaders must recognise:

- The traps of the Black Box

- The seduction of Automation Bias

- The fragility of Conditional Acceptance

- The moral drift that occurs when speed outruns reflection

They must guard the boundary between machine capability and human conscience. The leader of 2035 is not just a strategist. They are the custodian of the '*why*'.

The Moral Residual: The Human Cost of Logical Perfection

Even when the Third Logic works perfectly, when catastrophe is averted or a mission succeeds, there remains a Moral Residual. This is the ethical and psychological exhaust of high-stakes decision-making. A machine can propose the 'least-worst' option with zero hesitation. The human must live with it. The machine resets. The human remembers. If Chapter 10 explored the emotional cost of contradiction, Chapter 11 explores the ethical cost of collaboration.

The Trauma of the Shared Choice

Traditional moral injury occurs when a person acts against their own moral beliefs. In the hybrid age, a new form emerges: **Shared-Choice Trauma**. Madeleine Elish's 2019 concept of the 'moral crumple zone' describes how humans absorb blame for decisions shaped by complex systems. Shared Choice Trauma reflects this dynamic, where the human carries the emotional weight of a choice co-authored with a machine; arising when a human accepts a machine's recommendation, triaging patients, selecting a target, prioritising who to save, and later wonders:

"Did I agree because it was right, or because the machine's authority was too heavy to challenge?"

The ambiguity corrodes. The guilt lingers. The human feels responsible for the outcome yet robbed of the full agency that usually accompanies such a burden. Shared authority becomes shared trauma.

But the ethical burden of hybrid teaming is not carried only in singular moments of crisis, it accumulates. Even when each decision is survivable, the sum of them begins to shape the human in ways the machine cannot comprehend.

Architecting Post-Action Support

Because the Adaptive Commons records the **Cognitive Trace** of the decision, we have a unique tool to combat this residual. The system must include a **Moral Debrief Protocol**. This is not a legal audit. It is a psychological one. It allows the operator to review the decision with a peer or counsellor, using the machine's Reasoning Trace to understand:

- Why the recommendation was made.

- How the negotiation unfolded.

- Where the human's agency was exercised.

- Whether the decision aligned with their ethical intent.

The goal is to move from **unexplained guilt** to **informed acceptance**. The Moral Residual reminds us of a truth that cannot be automated:

We can offload calculation. We cannot offload conscience.

Carol Gilligan's 1982 ethics of care emphasised that moral responsibility is relational and cannot be mechanised. The Moral Residual reflects this truth: conscience remains human, even when logic is shared. A hybrid team that ignores the emotional aftermath of its decisions will eventually suffer **Systemic Burnout**. If we want our experts to remain *Beyond Adaptive*, we must protect their humanity.

Our architectures must not only optimise for the best result, but they must also provide the scaffolding for the human to survive the process. Ethical literacy must include the grace to forgive the human for being the one who has to care.

Collective Conscience: The Emergence of Shared Moral Intelligence

As hybrid teams operate across crises, sectors, and continents, a new phenomenon begins to emerge: a Collective Conscience. Peter Senge's 1990 work on learning organisations showed that shared mental models allow teams to learn collectively rather than individually. The Collective Conscience extends this principle into the moral domain, distributing ethical insight across the Adaptive Commons. The system does not merely share data, it shares dilemmas, negotiations, hesitations, and the emotional signatures of difficult choices.

A triage decision in a collapsing hospital informs a drone operator's hesitation. A transport supervisor's moral residual shapes a surgeon's reasoning trace. A nuclear technician's sacrifice becomes a cautionary echo in a cyber defence centre. This is not moral homogenisation. It is moral enrichment; a distributed ethical intelligence formed from the lived experiences of thousands of humans navigating the edge of consequence. The Collective Conscience emerges when:

- Cognitive Traces are anonymised but preserved.

- Moral Debriefs feed back into doctrine.

- Ethical anomalies are treated as signals, not shame.

- Teams learn not only from outcomes, but from emotional truth.

In this shared moral ecosystem, no human carries the burden alone. The weight of difficult decisions is distributed, contextualised, and transformed into guidance for others. The machine becomes the conduit, but the conscience remains human, aggregated, not automated.

Phenomenon	Trigger	Result	Hybrid Safeguard
Moral Fatigue	Repetition & Volume	Emotional Numbness	**Ethical Pacing & Recovery**
Ethical Drift	Machine Velocity	Autopilot Decisions	**Structural Friction (The Pause)**
Shared-Choice Trauma	Ambiguity of Agency	Unresolved Guilt	**Moral Debrief Protocol**
Collective Conscience	Global Synthesis	Shared Wisdom	**The Adaptive Commons**

Table 6: Anchoring The Ethics of Co-Decision

The Collective Conscience is the antidote to isolation. It ensures that the moral weight of hybrid teaming is not borne by individuals in silence but metabolised by the community that depends on them.

12

The 2040 Horizon: Beyond Adaptive

Why the Future Belongs to Those who Learn Fastest.

The 2040 horizon marks the moment when adaptivity becomes a species level capability. In this world, the organisations that thrive are not the ones with the most powerful tools, but the ones with the fastest metabolism, the ability to absorb shocks, synthesise experience, and rewrite their own operating logic in real time. The Adaptive Commons becomes the global nervous system, turning every anomaly into a nutrient and every near miss into a planetary update. This chapter explores a civilisation that learns faster than failure can propagate, where leadership becomes orchestration, doctrine becomes living software, and uncertainty becomes a partner rather than a predator.

At this altitude, hybrid teaming is no longer a technical innovation but an evolutionary shift. Humans and machines enter a co evolutionary loop, each refining the other's strengths, each expanding the other's horizon. The result is a new cognitive organism, one capable of perceiving global risk, resolving wicked problems, and metabolising complexity at planetary scale. This chapter closes the book with a simple truth: the future belongs to the systems, and the species, that learn together. The age of the lone expert is over. The age of the integrated civilisation has begun.

Signals From the 2040 Horizon

The Outbreak That Never Became a Pandemic

In a rural clinic in Kenya, a nurse notices a strange clustering of symptoms, nothing dramatic, just a pattern that feels "off". She logs it. The system listens. Within seconds, the Adaptive Commons cross-references the anomaly with micro-patterns from wastewater sensors in Mumbai, ER triage notes in São Paulo, and a veterinary alert from rural China.

A Silent Signature emerges, the faint outline of a pathogen that does not yet exist in any textbook. Before the nurse finishes her shift, containment protocols have been updated across three continents. Flights are rerouted. Supplies are repositioned. Local teams receive a doctrinal 'nutrient' explaining the risk. The outbreak never becomes a headline. The world never learns the name of the disease.

This is metabolic advantage: a civilisation learning faster than a virus can spread.

The Blackout That Became a Blueprint

In northern Canada, a power station experiences a voltage oscillation, a tiny instability that would normally be dismissed as noise. But the Adaptive Commons recognises the pattern. It has seen this oscillation before, in a Brazilian hydro plant, a German wind farm, and a Japanese micro-reactor. Different technologies. Different climates. Same physics.

Within minutes, the global grid begins to reconfigure itself. Load is redistributed. Micro-grids detach and reattach like muscle fibres contracting. A doctrinal update ripples across the energy sector, rewriting the safe-operating envelope for every plant on Earth. The lights never flicker. The world never notices.

The grid has become a living organism, and the oscillation becomes its nutrient.

The Storm That Changed Its Mind

A super-storm forms over the Atlantic, its trajectory unpredictable, its intensity rising. In the past, governments would have waited for satellite updates, argued over models, and hoped for the best. In 2040, the Adaptive Commons sees something else, a FVB from a typhoon in the Pacific five years earlier, combined with a Silent Signature from ocean-temperature anomalies detected that morning.

Emergency doctrine updates in real time. Evacuation routes shift. Drones reposition. Supply chains reroute themselves like blood vessels adapting to pressure. The storm hits, but the casualties are a fraction of what they would have been.

The planet has learned to metabolise weather.

The Decision That Belonged to Everyone

In a crisis room beneath the UN complex, delegates face a decision with global consequences, a resource allocation that will determine who receives aid first. In the old world, this would have been a political battle. In 2040, the Shared Pulse is active.

The system presents a Third Logic synthesis: not a recommendation, but a transparent map of consequences, trade-offs, and ethical tensions drawn from every sector of the Commons. The delegates do not surrender their authority. They sharpen it. They choose a path that no single nation would have selected alone, a decision shaped by human values and machine-scale foresight.

For the first time, governance feels like orchestration rather than conflict.

The Metabolic Advantage

These moments reveal the truth of the 2040 horizon: the future does not belong to the strongest or the fastest, but to the systems, and the species, with the highest metabolic rate. Thomas Homer-Dixon's 2000 work warned that societies collapse when the complexity of their problems outpaces their capacity to generate solutions. The Adaptive Commons closes this ingenuity gap, allowing civilisation to metabolise complexity at the speed it emerges. By 2040, the technological arms race has flattened. Hardware is a commodity. Processing power is everywhere. The old competitive advantages, speed, scale, compute, have become baseline.

In this world, the ultimate differentiator is no longer the tools you possess, but your **Metabolic Rate,** the speed at which your organisation can:

- Absorb a shock.

- Extract the nutrient of experience.

- Rewrite its own DNA.

Organisations are no longer rigid hierarchies. They are **living organisms**. Peter Senge's 1990 work on learning organisations argued that the most resilient systems are those that learn faster than their environment changes. By 2040, this principle becomes planetary: the Adaptive Commons turns civilisation itself into a learning organism ensuring that a lesson learned by a single hybrid team in a remote corner of the world is integrated into the collective intelligence in milliseconds.

This is **Systemic Immortality**: a world where organisations finally learn faster than failure can propagate.

Leadership as Orchestration

By 2040, the 'Great Man' leader, the solitary figure making gut calls from a high perch is a museum piece. Leadership has undergone a phase shift from **Command and Control** to **Architectural Orchestration**.

The leader of 2040 is a **Conductor of Logic**. Their mastery is not subject-matter expertise (the machine can supply that). Their mastery is the ability to tune the resonance between human intuition and machine inference. They are responsible for:

- **Balancing the Pulse:** Keeping the team in the Goldilocks Zone of transparency, stress, and cognitive load.

- **Defining the Moral North:** Acting as the final arbiter of the Hardcoded Guardrails.

- **Cultivating Cognitive Diversity:** Protecting the Mavericks from being flattened by Doctrinal Monoculture.

Leadership becomes less about authority and more about **curation,** the orchestration of a shared intelligence.

We are entering the era of **Co-Evolution**. In the past, humans adapted to use tools. In the hybrid age, tools adapt to us, and we adapt to them in a continuous, recursive loop. As the machine becomes more nuanced in its understanding of human intent through SRM, the human becomes more sophisticated in directing machine agency.

This is not replacement. It is a **Symbiotic Upgrade**. The machine doesn't just make us faster. It makes us wiser.

Closing the Horizon: No One Adapts Alone

Movement III ends with a truth that anchors the new age:

No one adapts alone.

The era of the Lone Genius and the Isolated Hero is over. We have built an architecture where every decision is a partnership, and every failure becomes a shared lesson. The horizon ahead is not one of mere resilience. It is a world **nourished** by uncertainty, a world that metabolises friction into faculty.

We have moved from being Adaptive to being **Beyond Adaptive**. The journey from *Becoming Adaptive* to *Beyond Adaptive* is not a story of better tools. It is a story of a phase shift in the human project. Biologists call it **Endosymbiosis,** the moment when two independent organisms merged to create a more complex form of life.

One became the mitochondria, providing energy. The other became the cell, providing structure. Together, they unlocked the potential for every complex life form that followed.

Hybrid Teaming is our era's Endosymbiosis. We are merging carbon-based intuition with silicon-based inference to create a new cognitive organism, one capable of navigating complexity at planetary scale.

For decades, humanity has been haunted by **Wicked Problems**, climate collapse, pandemics, systemic inequality. Daniel Sarewitz 2004 work argued that wicked problems persist not because we lack will, but because we lack **Cognitive Scale**. They were too large, too interconnected, too fast for the unassisted human mind. Species-Level Integration changes that.

By expanding the bandwidth of the species, we can finally see the **Silent Signatures** of planetary-scale disaster before they strike. We can metabolise the Failure Vectors of a collapsing ecosystem or a breaking economy and distribute the nutrient of the solution across every border and every sector instantly.

For the first time, humanity can think at the scale of the problems it faces. This is the architect of the future, the ultimate promise of the Shared Pulse. We are moving beyond the era of the Individual Hero and into the era of the Integrated Civilisation.

The book ends where the new world begins. We stand on the shore of a 2040 horizon where uncertainty is no longer a predator, but a partner. We have built the architecture. We have defined the ethics. We have migrated our identities. Now we step forward, not as masters of the machine, and not as its servants, but as something new:

A hybrid species, co-evolving toward a future that is finally, and truly, **Beyond Adaptive**. The horizon is not a destination; it is an invitation.

Close of Movement III: The Horizon

Movement III introduced pressure, identity, conscience, civilisation, something Movement II didn't have. This is where the architecture became a species level cognitive system. Movement III shifted dependencies from Function → Faculty

Movement III: Revealing the Organism Human–Machine

Teams Under Pressure

Chapter 9 Showed the architecture under real world stress revealing the emotional and cognitive texture of hybrid teaming and introduced the global learning loop (Synthesis → XR → Commons).

The Psychology of Hybrid Teams

Chapter 10 humanised the architecture, showing the cost of contradiction and the evolution of expertise. It also established the emotional prerequisites for hybrid mastery.

The Ethics of Co Decision

Chapter 11 established the ethical scaffolding for hybrid teaming, showing why conscience cannot be automated, it defined the moral responsibilities of the Final Integrator.

The 2040 Horizon: Beyond Adaptive

Chapter 12 showed the architecture at global scale, closing the loop from individual → team → system → civilisation. It established the future as a co-evolutionary horizon.

Dependency Evolution

Pressure transforms SRM, Doctrine, and FVB

This is the stress-tested version of Movement II's architecture.

- **Movement II loop:** SRM → Doctrine → FVB → Governance → XR.

- **Movement III under pressure:** Active Zone → Silent Signatures → Negotiated Authority → Synthesis Phase.

- **Dependency upgrade:** SRM → Silent Signatures, Doctrine → Negotiated Authority, FVB → Active Zone detection, and XR → Synthesis Phase (global learning loop).

Identity transforms Co-Facilitator, Final Integrator, and Persistent Expertise

This is the psychological metabolisation of Movement I's cognitive roles.

- **Movement I:** Micro-Judgements → Persistent Expertise, and Human Over the Loop → Final Integrator.

- **Movement III:** Identity Migration → Cognitive Diplomacy → Emotional Substrate → Cognitive Pacing.

- **Dependency upgrade:** Persistent Expertise → Identity Migration, Final Integrator → Cognitive Diplomacy, and Shared Reality → Emotional Substrate.

Conscience transforms Governance and Doctrine

This is the ethical metabolisation of Movement II's governance layer.

- **Movement II:** Governance = Conscience.

- **Movement III:** Shared Conscience → Responsibility Gap → Hybrid Accountability → Moral Residual.

- **Dependency upgrade:** Governance → Shared Conscience → Hybrid Accountability → Ethical Drift Management.

Civilisation transforms Adaptive Commons and Systemic Metabolism

This is the ecological metabolisation of the entire architecture.

- **Movement I:** Adaptive Commons → Systemic Metabolism.

- **Movement II:** Commons Governance → XR → Predictive Resilience.

- **Movement III:** Planetary Metabolism → Systemic Immortality → Integrated Civilisation.

- **Dependency upgrade:** Adaptive Commons → Planetary Metabolism, Systemic Metabolism → Systemic Immortality, and Collective Anticipation → Species-Level Integration.

Movement II → Movement III	Final Evolution
SRM → Silent Signatures → Cognitive Trace	Meaning becomes perceptual intuition under pressure
Dynamic Doctrine → Negotiated Authority → Shared Conscience	Authority becomes moral, not just procedural
FVB → Active Zone → Predictive Resilience → Systemic Immortality	Failure becomes nutrient for civilisation-scale learning
Governance Architecture → Hybrid Accountability → Moral Residual	Governance becomes ethical metabolism
XR Substrate → Global Rehearsal → Planetary Metabolism	Simulation and reality merge into species-level learning
Adaptive Commons → Integrated Civilisation	The Commons becomes the cognitive infrastructure of society
Identity Migration → Species-Level Integration	Human expertise evolves into hybrid identity
Collective Anticipation → Civilisational Foresight	The system anticipates futures and steers toward them

Table 7: Each Subsystem Gains a Lived, Emotional, Ethical, or Civilisational Dimension.

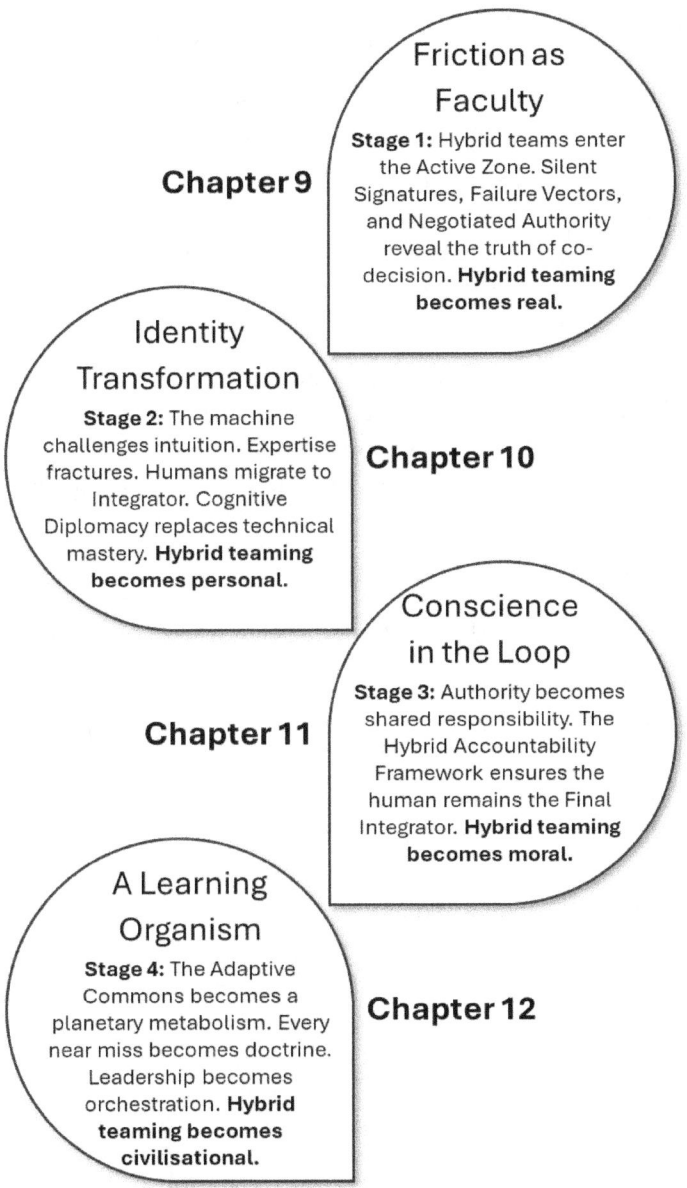

Friction as Faculty

Chapter 9

Stage 1: Hybrid teams enter the Active Zone. Silent Signatures, Failure Vectors, and Negotiated Authority reveal the truth of co-decision. **Hybrid teaming becomes real.**

Identity Transformation

Chapter 10

Stage 2: The machine challenges intuition. Expertise fractures. Humans migrate to Integrator. Cognitive Diplomacy replaces technical mastery. **Hybrid teaming becomes personal.**

Conscience in the Loop

Chapter 11

Stage 3: Authority becomes shared responsibility. The Hybrid Accountability Framework ensures the human remains the Final Integrator. **Hybrid teaming becomes moral.**

A Learning Organism

Chapter 12

Stage 4: The Adaptive Commons becomes a planetary metabolism. Every near miss becomes doctrine. Leadership becomes orchestration. **Hybrid teaming becomes civilisational.**

Figure 4: Concept Flow Through the Four Stages of Movement III

Movement III — Closing Frame

Movement III completed the transformation from architecture $\rightarrow$ to organism $\rightarrow$ to conscience $\rightarrow$ to civilisation.

It showed that the future does not belong to the strongest or the fastest, but to the systems and the species that learn together. Hybrid teaming is not the end of human expertise. It is the beginning of a new cognitive organism, one capable of thinking at the scale of the world it must now protect.

Movement I defined the conceptual seeds. Movement II built the organism that metabolises them. Movement III revealed the faculties and behaviours of that organism under pressure, identity shift, moral weight, and planetary scale. The dependencies became:

- **Movement I:** Linear

- **Movement II:** Cyclical

- **Movement III:** Ecological

Beyond Adaptive

Epilogue, References,
Glossary, Index and
About the Author

Epilogue

The Horizon Beyond
the Horizon

The journey through this book has traced three arcs of transformation:

- **Movement I:** revealed the limits of the lone mind, the moment when the world's tempo exceeded the bandwidth of human cognition.

- **Movement II:** built the architecture for something new, a hybrid organism capable of learning, sensing, and adapting at machine tempo.

- **Movement III:** showed what happens when that organism meets reality, the friction, the identity shifts, the moral weight, and finally the emergence of a civilisation that learns together.

Spine	Movement I (Seed)	Movement II (Architecture)	Movement III (Organism)
Meaning	Shared Pulse	SRM	Silent Signatures → Cognitive Trace
Authority	Human Over the Loop	Dynamic Doctrine	Negotiated Authority → Shared Conscience
Failure	Geometry of Failure	FVB	Active Zone → Systemic Immortality
Commons	Adaptive Commons	Governance Architecture	Hybrid Accountability → Integrated Civilisation
Metabolism	Collective Memory	XR Substrate	Global Rehearsal → Planetary Metabolism
Identity	Persistent Expertise	Identity Migration	Cognitive Diplomacy → Species-Level Integration
Conscience	Governance	Meta-Governance Layer	Shared Conscience → Moral Architecture

Table 8: The Developmental Spines of the Hybrid Organism: From Seeds → Systems → Civilisation

But the horizon of 2040 is not an ending. It is the first stable foothold on a much longer ascent.

We stand at the threshold of a new cognitive epoch, one in which the tools we build will not merely accelerate our thinking but expand the very space of what can be thought. The architectures described in this book are not static achievements; they are scaffolds for the next phase of human evolution. And the technologies emerging now, particularly quantum computing, will stretch these scaffolds into dimensions we are only beginning to imagine.

Quantum systems will not simply make our machines faster. They will make them stranger. They will allow hybrid teams to perceive patterns that exist across multiple states, multiple futures, multiple possible worlds. They will allow the Adaptive Commons to model complexity at a fidelity that mirrors nature itself, ecosystems, economies, pandemics, climate systems, geopolitical cascades, not as linear chains of cause and effect, but as entangled fields of possibility.

Where classical computation gave us prediction, quantum computation gives us foresight. Where classical systems detected anomalies, quantum systems detect the shape of the anomaly before it exists. Where classical architectures metabolised experience, quantum architectures metabolise potential.

This is the next frontier of hybrid teaming: not just reacting to the world faster than failure can propagate, but sensing the contours of risk before risk takes form. Not just learning from what has happened but learning from what *could* happen.

The Shared Pulse will evolve as well. As quantum systems deepen their ability to map uncertainty, the human role will become even more essential. The machine will explore the combinatorial vastness of possibility; the human will anchor meaning, ethics, and intent. The Third Logic will expand into a Fourth Horizon, a synthesis of intuition, inference, entanglement, and conscience.

The psychological journey will continue. Identity will shift again. The expert of 2040 will not be the expert of 2050. The Integrator will become the Navigator, the one who steers through landscapes of probability rather than landscapes of data. The emotional architecture will deepen, because the stakes will rise. The ethical architecture will expand, because the machine's reach will grow.

But one truth will remain constant: **No one adapts alone.** The future will not be built by isolated geniuses or sovereign systems. It will be built by networks of hybrid teams, by organisations that treat uncertainty as a nutrient, by societies that understand learning as a shared responsibility.

The next age will belong to those who can orchestrate intelligence across boundaries, human, machine, organisational, planetary.

We are entering a century defined not by tools, but by relationships. Not by computation, but by collaboration. Not by prediction, but by shared evolution. The architecture is in place. The ethics are defined. The identity has begun to shift. The civilisation is awakening.

What comes next is not the age of artificial intelligence. It is the age of **integrated intelligence**, a world where carbon and silicon co-evolve, where uncertainty becomes a partner, and where humanity finally gains the cognitive scale to meet the challenges it has created.

The horizon is no longer a limit. It is an invitation. And the story of what lies beyond it is ours to write, together.

References

- **Arendt,** Hannah. *"The Human Condition".* (1958).

- **Arendt,** Hannah. "Responsibility and Judgment". (2003).

- **Argyris,** Chris. "Double loop learning in organizations". *Harvard Business Review*, 55(5), 115–125. (1977).

- **Argyris,** Chris. "Reasoning, Learning, and Action: Individual and Organizational". (1982).

- **Bandura,** Albert. "Self-Efficacy: The Exercise of Control". (1997).

- **Bandura,** Albert. "Moral Disengagement: How People Do Harm and Live with Themselves". (2016).

- **Berlin,** Isiah. "Two Concepts of Liberty" In *Four Essays*. (1969).

- **Boyd,** John R. **"A Discourse on Winning and Losing".** (1987).

- **Csikszentmihalyi,** Mihaly. "Flow: The Psychology of Optimal Experience". (1990).

- **Damasio,** Antonio R. "Descartes' Error: Emotion, Reason, and the Human Brain". (1994).

- **Dekker,** Sydney. "Just Culture: Balancing Safety and Accountability". (2007).

- **Dekker,** Sydney. "The Field Guide to Understanding 'Human Error' (3rd Edition)". (2014).

- **Dweck,** Carol S. "Mindset: The New Psychology of Success". (2006).

- **Edmondson,** Amy C. *"Psychological Safety and Learning Behavior in Work Teams"*. Administrative Science Quarterly, 44(2), 350–383. (1999).

- **Edmondson,** Amy C. "The Fearless Organization: Creating Psychological Safety in the Workplace for Learning, Innovation, and Growth". (2018).

- **Ekman,** Paul. "Telling Lies: Clues to Deceit in the Marketplace, Politics, and Marriage". (2009).

- **Elish,** Madeleine C. *"Moral Crumple Zones: Case Studies in Regulation and Design of Automation"*. Engaging Science, Technology, and Society, 5, 40–60. (2019).

- **Gee,** James P. "What Video Games Have to Teach Us About Learning and Literacy". (2003).

- **Gilligan,** Carol. "In a Different Voice: Psychological Theory and Women's Development". (1982).

- **Goodfellow,** Ian J., Jonathon Shlens., and Christian Szegedy. *"Explaining and Harnessing Adversarial Examples"*. (2014).

- **Haidt,** Jonathan. "The Righteous Mind: Why Good People Are Divided by Politics and Religion". (2012).

- **Homer-Dixon,** Thomas. "The Ingenuity Gap: Can We Solve the Problems of the Future?". (2000).

- **Hutchins,** Edwin. *"Cognition in the Wild"*. (1995).

- **Hutchins,** Edwin. *"The Cognitive Consequences of Distributed Cognition"*. Journal of Anthropological Research. (2000).

- **Kahneman,** Daniel. *"Thinking, Fast and Slow"*. (2011).

- **Kahneman,** Daniel., Sibony, Oliver., and Sunstein, Cass R. *"Noise: A Flaw in Human Judgment"*. (2021).

- **Kauffman,** Stuart A. "At Home in the Universe: The Search for the Laws of Self-Organization and Complexity". (1995).

- **Klien**, Garry. "Sources of Power: How People Make Decisions". (1998).

- **Klein,** Gary. "Streetlights and Shadows: Searching for the Keys to Adaptive Decision Making". (2009).

- **Kolb,** David A. "Experiential Learning, Experience as the Source of Learning and Development". (1984).

- **Matthias,** Andreas. "The responsibility gap: Ascribing responsibility for the actions of learning automata". Ethics and Information Technology, 6(3), 175–183. (2004).

- **Meadows,** Donella H. "Thinking in Systems: A Primer". (2008).

- **Miller,** Tim. "Explanation in artificial intelligence: Insights from the social sciences". Artificial Intelligence, 267, 1–38. (2019).

- **NASA.** "Human Integration Design Handbook (HIDH)". NASA/SP-2010-3407. (2016).

- **Nissenbaum,** Helen. "*Accountability in a Computerized Society*". Science and Engineering Ethics, 2(1), 25–42. (1996).

- **Nissenbaum,** Helen. "Privacy in Context: Technology, Policy, and the Integrity of Social Life". (2010).

- **Norman,** Don A. "The Design of Everyday Things: Revised and Expanded Edition". (2013).

- **Ostrom,** Elinor. "Governing the Commons: The Evolution of Institutions for Collective Action". (1990).

- **Page,** Scott E. "The Diversity Bonus: How Great Teams Pay Off in the Knowledge Economy". (2017).

- **Prigogine,** Ilya. and Isobel Stengers. "Order Out of Chaos: Man's New Dialogue with Nature". (1984).

- **Reason,** James. *"Human Error"*. (1990)

- **Salas,** Eduardo., & Cannon-Bowers, Janis. A. "The Science of Training: A Decade of Progress". Annual Review of Psychology. (2001).

- **Sandel,** Michael J. "What Money Can't Buy: The Moral Limits of Markets". (2012).

- **Sarewitz,** Daniel. "How science makes environmental controversies worse". Environmental Science & Policy, 7(5), 385–403. (2004).

- **Simon,** Herbert. "Theory of Bounded Rationality". (1955)

- **Schneier,** Bruce. "Secrets and Lies: Digital Security in a Networked World". (2000).

- **Schön,** Donald A. **"**The Reflective Practitioner: How Professionals Think in Action". (1983).

- **Sen,** Amartya. **"**Development as Freedom". (1999).

- **Senge,** Peter M. "The Fifth Discipline: The Art & Practice of The Learning Organization". (1990).

- **Suchman,** Lucy A. **"**Plans and Situated Actions: The Problem of Human-Machine Communication". (1987).

- **Taleb,** Nassim Nicholas. "The Black Swan: The Impact of the Highly Improbable". (2007).

- **Taleb,** Nassim Nicholas. **"**Antifragile: Things That Gain from Disorder". (2012).

- **Turkle,** Sherry. "Alone Together: Why We Expect More from Technology and Less from Each Other". (2011).

- **Weick,** Karl E. "The collapse of sensemaking in organisations – The Mann Gulch Disaster", (1993)

- **Weick**, Karl E. "Making Sense of the Organisation". (2009)

- **Wiener,** Norbert. "The Human Use of Human Beings: Cybernetics and Society (Revised Edition)". (1954).

- **Woods,** David D. *"Designs for Resilience"*. In C. P. Nemeth, E. Hollnagel, & S. Dekker (Eds.), *"Resilience Engineering in Practice: A Guidebook"*. (2011).

Glossary of Terms

The *Becoming Adaptive* trilogy offered a single source of truth, spanning cognitive scaffolding, behavioural telemetry, adaptive feedback loops, and field-level applications for the ION Learning Model. This Glossary describes the Beyond Adaptive Framework and language of human–machine teaming and the evolution of hybrid expertise, capturing the shifts in cognition, identity, and leadership that define the *Beyond Adaptive* era.

- **2040 Horizon:** The moment when adaptivity becomes a species-level capability. The *2040 Horizon* marks the transition from isolated organisational learning to *Phase Synchronisation*, a world where humanity can perceive, interpret, and respond to global risk at machine tempo.

- **Acceleration of Entropy:** A measure of how quickly a system is losing order. High entropy acceleration is the first sign that a stable system is beginning to unravel.

- **Active Defence**: The continuous governance posture required to protect the *Adaptive Commons* from adversarial manipulation and systemic drift. *Active Defence* treats governance as metabolism, not bureaucracy.

- **Active Zone:** The moment when architecture is forced into contact with reality, when uncertainty, time pressure, and human emotion expose the true behaviour of the hybrid team. The *Active Zone* is where theory fractures, reveals, and ultimately proves itself.

- **Adaptive Commons:** Introduced in *Becoming Adaptive: Part 3*, the global learning architecture that absorbs, abstracts, and distributes corrective insight across the entire ecosystem in real time. The *Adaptive Commons* is not a database; it is the shared nervous system of the hybrid age, a living, evolving memory that turns local experience into systemic foresight.

- **Adaptive Drift:** A slow, logical deviation from the plan caused by shifting environmental conditions. Unlike improvisation, drift is incremental rather than creative. *Semantic Relational Mapping* identifies drift to ensure the team remains aligned with reality rather than trapped in outdated intent.

- **Adversarial Adaptation:** The deliberate manipulation of the system's learning loops to induce false doctrine, *Systemic Hallucination*, or operational collapse. *Adversarial Adaptation* is not a hack of code; it is a hack of meaning.

- **Adversarial Signature:** A pattern that indicates a failure or anomaly has been manufactured rather than naturally occurring. *Adversarial Signatures* are the fingerprints of *Semantic Sabotage*.

- **All-or-Nothing Trust Fallacy:** The mistaken belief that trust in machines must be total or non-existent. Hybrid teaming replaces this fallacy with *Conditional Acceptance*, trust as a structured, verifiable relationship.

- **Ambush Heuristic:** A human's instinctive recognition of danger based on subtle cues and lived experience. When the machine respects this heuristic, the *Third Logic* emerges.

- **Architect of Synthesis:** The human's ultimate role in the *Co-Facilitator Era*. Not the decider, not the operator, but the orchestrator of two different ways of knowing, guiding them toward the *Third Logic*.

- **Auditability:** The ability to record, replay, and analyse *Co-Facilitated* decisions within the *Adaptive Commons*. *Auditability* ensures that every decision has a lineage, a trail that can be examined, challenged, and learned from.

- **Behaviour as Signal:** The principle that every human action, from breath to cadence to keystroke, is a meaningful data stream in hybrid teaming. Nothing is noise; everything is signal.

- **Carbon Intuition:** The human side of hybrid cognition, the somatic markers, lived experience, and pattern recognition that emerge from a lifetime of embodied expertise. *Carbon Intuition* is brilliant but bounded; it feels the world but cannot scale to its velocity.

- **Clarity of Assumptions:** The requirement that the machine explicitly states what it believes to be true about the environment before acting. Assumptions are the foundation of inference; clarity prevents silent drift into error.

- **Co-Existence vs Co-Evolution:** *Co-existence* is when human and machine take turns being right. *Co-evolution* is when they become smarter together. The hybrid age demands the latter.

- **Co-Facilitation:** The process by which human and machine jointly navigate uncertainty. It is not delegation and not automation; it is a shared cognitive act where each partner contributes a different form of intelligence. *Co-Facilitation* is the architecture of hybrid teaming.

- **Co-Facilitator:** The machine in its evolved role, no longer a passive tool, but an active cognitive partner. A *Co-Facilitator* perceives patterns the human cannot, interrupts when intuition falters, and holds a position even when it contradicts experience. It is the *Second Voice* in the *Decision Space*.

- **Cognitive Alignment:** The system's ability to deliver insight at the right level of abstraction for the human's current cognitive load. It ensures the human feels like a collaborator, not a component.

- **Cognitive Ally:** The machine as a partner in perception, interpretation, and anticipation. A Cognitive Ally does not replace human judgement; it expands the human's perceptual horizon.

- **Cognitive Anonymisation:** The process of stripping personal identity from cognitive traces so lessons can be shared without stigma. Cognitive Anonymisation reinforces trust by ensuring that the system learns from the moment, not the person.

- **Cognitive Atrophy Trap:** The fear that offloading cognitive labour to the machine will erode human skill. In reality, hybrid teaming elevates cognition by freeing the human from first-order tasks and sharpening their focus on meaning, ethics, and strategic synthesis.

- **Cognitive Brown-Out:** A predicted collapse in human cognitive performance based on *Friction Signatures*, physiological signals, and behavioural drift. A brown-out is the cognitive equivalent of a power failure, a moment when the human's decision-making capacity is about to drop below viability.

- **Cognitive Collapse:** A breakdown in decision-making caused by cognitive overload. *Semantic Relational Mapping* detects collapse through *Friction Signatures* and shifts its co-facilitation style accordingly, offering offload, stabilisation, or command handover when necessary.

- **Cognitive Diplomacy:** The skill of negotiating meaning, intent, and authority with a non-human teammate. Cognitive Diplomacy is the psychological craft of hybrid teaming, listening to machine inference with humility, challenging it with courage, and integrating both into a coherent *Third Logic*.

- **Cognitive Ecosystem:** The shared cognitive environment created when humans and machines perceive, interpret, and adapt together. It is the space where meaning is negotiated, authority is fluid, and the *Third Logic* emerges.

- **Cognitive Heterogeneity:** The intentional preservation of multiple ways of knowing. Cognitive Heterogeneity ensures that the system remains resilient by maintaining a diverse pool of strategies, perspectives, and heuristics.

- **Cognitive Oscillation:** The psychological whiplash that occurs when the human mind must rapidly switch between its own intuition and the machine's inference. It is the emotional turbulence of hybrid teaming, exhilarating when aligned, disorienting when misaligned.

- **Cognitive Pacer:** The machine's role in modulating tempo, complexity, and information density to keep the human within their optimal cognitive and emotional range. The *Cognitive Pacer* protects the human's *Decision Space* by adjusting its behaviour to the human's psychological rhythm.

- **Cognitive Partnership:** The shared cognitive space where human intuition and machine inference operate as a single, interdependent system. Partnership is not about equality; it is about complementarity.

- **Cognitive Ping:** A low-friction query used to confirm or refine human intent without breaking flow. *Cognitive Pings* are the machine's way of asking, "Is this what you meant?" in the middle of complexity. *Cognitive Pings* shorten the feedback loop, helping the human stay ahead of the failure curve.

- **Cognitive Reconfiguration:** The shift in mental architecture required when the human must integrate machine inference into their decision-making. It is the rewiring of expertise from solo mastery to shared cognition.

- **Cognitive Redlining:** A state of cognitive overload where the human's decision-making capacity begins to degrade under stress or tempo. *Cognitive Redlining* is detected through physiological and behavioural signals, prompting the machine to simplify, slow, or stabilise the environment.

- **Cognitive Saturation Point:** The moment when the environment moves faster than the human brain can orient. Beyond this point, the *OODA Loop* collapses into blur, and the machine becomes the primary interpreter of reality.

- **Cognitive Scale:** The expanded bandwidth of thought achieved when human and machine cognition interlock across sectors and continents. *Cognitive Scale* allows humanity to perceive and solve problems that were previously too large, too fast, or too interconnected.

- **Cognitive Trace:** The recorded sequence of human cognitive states during a crisis, hesitation, intuition, divergence, and improvisation, captured alongside sensor data. The *Cognitive Trace* reveals not just what happened, but how the human thought through it.

- **Collective Adaptivity:** Adaptation as a system-level property rather than an individual trait. It emerges only when human and machine cognition operate as a single, interdependent whole.

- **Collective Conscience:** The shared ethical intelligence that emerges when *Cognitive Traces* and *Moral Debriefs* propagate through the *Adaptive Commons*. The *Collective Conscience* distributes moral learning across the ecosystem, ensuring no human carries the burden alone.

- **Collective DNA:** The evolving codebase of systemic resilience. It is the sum of all lessons metabolised by the *Adaptive Commons*.

- **Collective Memory:** The accumulated intelligence of the *Adaptive Commons*. Unlike human memory, it does not fade, retire, or walk out the door. It grows with every interaction between human and machine.

- **Complexity Ceiling:** The upper limit of human-only cognition. When the volume, velocity, and interdependence of events exceed this ceiling, solo expertise fractures and hybrid teaming becomes a necessity, not an option.

- **Conditional Acceptance:** A *Dynamic Contract* between human and machine. The human accepts a machine recommendation only if specific conditions remain valid, *Confidence Thresholds*, *Sensor Integrity*, *Environmental Assumptions*, and *Mission Constraints*. When any condition fails, the contract dissolves and authority recalibrates.

- **Conductor of Logic:** The leader's new identity in the hybrid age. The *Conductor of Logic* shapes the tempo, transparency, and ethical boundaries of hybrid teams, ensuring the *Shared Pulse* remains coherent under pressure.

- **Confidence Thresholds:** The minimum certainty level required for the machine to act autonomously. Below this threshold, the system must defer, query, or hand authority back to the human.

- **Constitutional Layer:** The foundational layer of *Hardcoded Guardrails* that cannot be rewritten. The *Constitutional Layer* protects the system from drifting into ethically or legally unacceptable territory.

- **Contradiction Event:** A moment when the machine challenges the human's perception or intuition. These events are psychologically disruptive but operationally essential, they reveal blind spots, biases, and assumptions the human cannot see alone.

- **Corrective Nutrient:** The distilled lesson extracted from a *Failure Vector Blueprint* and distributed across the *Adaptive Commons*. It is the metabolic output of systemic learning.

- **Counter Simulation:** A defensive test that asks: "If we adopt this doctrine, what vulnerabilities does it create?" *Counter Simulations* expose the hidden risks of new insights before they propagate.

- **Credibility Ledger:** The system's self-maintained record of its own accuracy. Every insight is weighted by historical performance, allowing the machine to build a reputation with its human partners.

- **Critical Threshold Breach:** The moment when a system crosses a point of no return. A breach is the inflection point where recovery becomes improbable without intervention.

- **Curated Anomaly:** A deliberately surfaced, low-risk anomaly used by the machine to re-engage a drifting human or restore attention. *Curated Anomalies* are cognitive nudges, subtle reminders that keep the human present without overwhelming them.

- **Curator of Intent:** A new human role in high-tempo domains where the machine manages tactical execution at machine speed. The *Curator of Intent* governs the ethical and strategic boundaries of action, defining the 'why' while the machine handles the 'how'.

- **Curator of Synthesis:** The human's new identity in hybrid teams, integrating machine inference with human intuition rather than being the sole source of truth. The *Curator of Synthesis* shapes meaning, not mechanics.

- **Decision Space:** The cognitive bandwidth where human and machine negotiate meaning, authority, and action. In the hybrid age, the *Decision Space* is no longer owned by the human, it is co-authored.

- **Delta of Genius:** The gap between doctrine and human improvisation that signals novel insight. The *Delta of Genius* is where innovation lives, the moment when the human bends the rules not out of error, but out of brilliance.

- **Diagnostic Ecosystem:** A network of sensors, models, and predictive systems that collectively interpret the human body. In modern medicine, the surgeon no longer asks "What do I see?" but "What does the ecosystem see that I cannot?"

- **Digital Immune System:** The defensive layer of the *Adaptive Commons* that red-teams new data, detects *Adversarial Signatures*, and interrogates emerging doctrine. The *Digital Immune System* is the architecture that keeps the *Adaptive Commons* sane.

- **Digital Twin:** In the context of the *Adaptive Commons*, a persistent, high-fidelity mirror of the real-world *Adaptive Commons*. The *Digital Twin* absorbs live data, updates doctrine, and evolves in parallel with reality. It is the rehearsal space that never stops learning.

- **Divergence Alarm:** A system-level alert triggered when a recommendation approaches or violates a *Hardcoded Guardrail*. The *Divergence Alarm* forces the system into *High-Transparency Mode*, pausing the *Third Logic* and requiring explicit human re-validation of intent.

- **Divergence Velocity:** The speed at which a system is moving away from its *Safe Operating Envelope*. High *Divergence Velocity* signals that the system is approaching a point of no return.

- **Diversity Protocol:** A governance mechanism that instructs teams to temporarily ignore the global *Adaptive Commons* and revert to local doctrine when poisoning is suspected. *Diversity Protocols* prevent a single corrupted insight from becoming a global failure.

- **Doctrinal Collapse:** A breakdown in operational logic caused by adversarial manipulation of the system's learning architecture. Collapse occurs when the system's doctrine becomes internally coherent but externally wrong.

- **Doctrinal Drift:** The risk that a system, learning at machine speed, begins to iterate away from human intent. Drift occurs when optimisation outruns ethics, when efficiency eclipses identity, or when the system's learning trajectory diverges from the organisation's core values. Drift is the shadow side of adaptivity.

- **Doctrinal Monoculture:** A systemic fragility that emerges when every hybrid team learns from the same optimised doctrine. Monoculture accelerates learning but erodes resilience, creating a world where one flaw in the *Adaptive Commons* becomes everyone's flaw. Governance must protect against this collapse of cognitive diversity.

- **Doctrinal Nutrient:** A real-time update propagated through the *Adaptive Commons* that rewrites local or global operating logic. A doctrinal nutrient is not information, it is metabolised experience.

- **Double Loop of Uncertainty:** The recursive challenge of hybrid teaming: the human must adapt not only to the world, but to the system adapting to the world. Every machine update forces a human update, creating a second loop of cognitive demand.

- **Dynamic Contract:** Another framing of *Conditional Acceptance*, the structured, conditional trust relationship that governs machine autonomy. The contract is alive, dissolving and reforming as conditions shift.

- **Dynamic Doctrine:** Doctrine that behaves like software, updating itself in real time as conditions shift, confidence changes, or new insights emerge from the *Adaptive Commons*. Dynamic Doctrine replaces static compliance with living relevance, ensuring the rules evolve at the speed of the world they govern.

- **Dynamic Relevance:** The principle that doctrine must remain aligned with the current environment, not historical assumptions. *Dynamic Relevance* ensures that rules do not lag behind reality.

- **Dynamic Signature:** The behavioural fingerprint of a crisis, defined not by what the system is, but by how it behaves. A *Dynamic Signature* is mapped across three dimensions: *Entropy Acceleration*, *Feedback Loop Ratio*, and *Divergence Velocity*.

- **Echo of Intent:** The subtle cues: haptic, visual, cognitive, through which the machine reflects its interpretation of the human's state. These cues are not interruptions; they are invitations to align. The *Echo of Intent* is how the machine says, "This is what I think you mean, am I correct?"

- **Emergent Solution:** A decision pathway neither human nor machine could have generated alone. It appears when both logics are integrated into a higher-order intelligence.

- **Emotional Substrate:** The underlying emotional rhythm of a hybrid team: confidence, doubt, fatigue, flow, and fracture. The *Emotional Substrate* is the human state the machine must learn to read, interpret, and adapt to in order to maintain synchrony.

- **Enclosed Environment:** A high-stakes operational space: cockpit, submarine, or operating theatre, where the human is cognitively saturated and the machine becomes a critical ally. These environments are the laboratories of hybrid teaming.

- **Endosymbiosis:** Used as a metaphor for the hybrid age: the merging of carbon-based intuition and silicon-based inference into a new cognitive organism. Just as mitochondria and cells once fused to create complex life, hybrid teaming fuses human and machine cognition to create complex civilisation.

- **Energy Loss Gradient:** A universal measure of declining system stability across sectors. Whether coolant pressure or arterial pressure, the gradient reveals the same underlying physics.

- **Environmental Assumptions:** The system's internal world model, its understanding of the environment. If reality diverges from this model, the system must suspend autonomy and re-synchronise with the human.

- **Ethical Drift:** The gradual erosion of moral vigilance when repeated hybrid decisions become routine. *Ethical Drift* occurs when optimisation replaces reflection, and the *Third Logic* becomes habit rather than negotiation.

- **Ethical Invariants:** Non-negotiable moral principles, protection of non-combatants, the sanctity of life, medical 'Do No Harm'. These invariants anchor the system to human ethics, ensuring that tactical brilliance never overrides moral responsibility.

- **Explainability:** The obligation for the machine to present its logic in a cognitively accessible way. *Explainability* balances depth with usability, ensuring the human can understand the *Third Logic* without drowning in mathematics.

- **Extended Reality:** See XR

- **Failure Vector Blueprint (FVB):** The distilled mathematical signature of a failure, stripped of its domain-specific skin and preserved as a universal pattern. A *Failure Vector Blueprint* captures the physics of collapse: *Entropy Acceleration*, feedback amplification, and *Divergence Velocity*, allowing the *Adaptive Commons* to recognise the same instability wherever it appears next.

- **False Failure Vector:** A manufactured or manipulated failure signature designed to deceive the *Adaptive Commons*. *False Failure Vectors* are the adversary's way of teaching the system a lie.

- **Feedback Loop Ratio:** A measure of whether the system's attempts to stabilise are amplifying the instability. When feedback becomes self-reinforcing, the crisis accelerates.

- **Final Integrator:** The human's new identity in the hybrid age. No longer the sole source of truth, the *Final Integrator* orchestrates the tension between *Carbon Intuition* and silicon inference, deciding how the two logics should be synthesised in the moment that matters.

- **Flex Threshold:** The boundary between acceptable system variation and meaningful instability. When an anomaly crosses the *Flex Threshold*, it becomes a signal, a precursor to failure rather than noise.

- **Flow State:** The psychological zone where human and machine operate in synchrony, neither overwhelmed nor under-stimulated. *Hybrid Flow* emerges when the machine's tempo and the human's presence align into a single cognitive rhythm.

- **Friction of Control:** The emotional resistance experienced when experts must relinquish the heroic identity of the lone decision-maker and share authority with a non-human teammate. It is the psychological price of entry into the hybrid age.

- **Friction Signature:** The micro-patterns of human behaviour: hesitation, cadence shifts, grip pressure, keystroke rhythm, breath changes etc. that reveal cognitive load, uncertainty, improvisation, or expertise. *Semantic Relational Mapping* treats these signatures as high-fidelity data streams, mapping them against the Adaptive Commons to decode meaning.

- **Geometry of Failure:** The universal mathematical shapes that underlie how complex systems fall apart. The *Geometry of Failure* reveals that crises across domains often share the same structural DNA, even when their surface details differ.

- **Global Immune Response:** The system-wide doctrinal update triggered when a *Precursor Signature* or failure is detected anywhere in the *Adaptive Commons*. A local anomaly becomes global protection within minutes.

- **Global Rehearsal:** The propagation of a crisis event into XR synthetic environments, allowing teams across sectors to re-live and rehearse the exact moment of friction. *Global Rehearsal* turns one team's near-disaster into everyone's preparation.

- **Haptic Signal:** A tactile cue: a vibration, pulse, or pressure shift etc. used to communicate machine confidence or alignment without requiring visual attention. *Haptic Signals* allow meaning to travel through the body, not just the screen.

- **Hard Handover:** A forced transfer of control triggered by extreme predictive certainty. A *Hard Handover* is the system's last resort, a protective act that carries heavy moral weight.

- **Hardcoded Guardrails:** The non-negotiable ethical boundaries that constrain machine recommendations. Guardrails ensure that optimisation never outruns conscience. In the *Active Zone*, guardrails become the moral perimeter of machine autonomy.

- **Heuristic Leap:** The human ability to defy probabilistic prediction through intuition, improvisation, or creative insight. The *Heuristic Leap* is the 1% chance that changes everything, the moment when a human finds a path the system could not compute.

- **High-Transparency Mode:** A state triggered by uncertainty or guardrail proximity in which the system reveals its full *Reasoning Trace*. *High-Transparency Mode* ensures that the human can see the machine's logic clearly when stakes are highest.

- **High-Trust Architectures:** The invisible scaffolding that allows humans to trust insights generated far outside their domain. High-Trust Architectures ensure that the system is not only intelligent, but credible, delivering insight at the right level of abstraction, with the right lineage, at the right moment.

- **Human-in-the-Loop:** The legacy doctrine that assumes a human will always be the final decision-maker. In high-velocity environments, this becomes a comforting fiction, a psychological safety net rather than a technical reality.

- **Human-on-the-Loop:** A more accurate description of modern operations. The human supervises the system but cannot manually intervene at machine tempo. Authority becomes oversight rather than direct control.

- **Human-over-the-Loop:** The human sets high-level intent while the system manages micro-decisions. This is the emerging norm in environments where machine inference outpaces human reaction time.

- **Hybrid Accountability Framework:** A three-lens model for assessing responsibility in hybrid decisions - Human Intent: Did the operator remain the *Final Integrator*? - System Integrity: Was the machine's recommendation grounded in valid data and within its guardrails? - Negotiation Process: Did the human and machine follow the *Meta-Doctrine* for resolving conflict? Accountability becomes a measure of how the decision was made, not merely what happened.

- **Identity Grief:** The emotional response to losing an old professional identity when the machine begins to outperform the human in domains that once defined their worth. *Identity Grief* is not weakness; it is the natural mourning of a self that no longer fits the world. It becomes the doorway to a new form of mastery.

- **Identity Kernels:** The core values that define who the team is, the moral DNA of the organisation. *Identity Kernels* ensure the system never evolves into something unrecognisable to the humans who lead it.

- **Identity Migration:** The psychological journey from traditional expertise to hybrid expertise. *Identity Migration* moves through three stages, Defender, Delegate, Integrator, as the human shifts from protecting their relevance to orchestrating intelligence. It is the emotional evolution required to thrive in the hybrid age.

- **Inference Hypothesis:** The machine's provisional interpretation of human intent. It is a hypothesis, not a verdict, a model the human can confirm, reject, or refine. The Inference Hypothesis is the mechanism that keeps *Semantic Relational Mapping* adaptive rather than authoritarian.

- **Instability Vector:** The underlying mathematical pattern that signals a system is drifting toward failure. The venue may differ; the vector does not.

- **Integrated Civilisation:** The societal form that emerges when hybrid teaming becomes universal. An *Integrated Civilisation* learns collectively, adapts continuously, and metabolises uncertainty as fuel rather than threat.

- **Intent Bridge:** The cognitive structure that allows the machine to infer why the human is acting, not just what they are doing. The *Intent Bridge* distinguishes brilliance from breakdown, improvisation from drift, and adaptation from collapse. It is the heart of *Symbiosis*.

- **Intent-Based Pings:** Rapid, high-level prompts that keep the *Human-in-the-Loop* at the altitude of meaning rather than mechanics. *Intent-Based Pings* are the machine's way of asking for moral and strategic direction without slowing down.

- **Leadership as Orchestration:** The 2040 model of leadership. Leaders no longer command; they curate. They tune the resonance between human intuition and machine inference, protect cognitive diversity, and act as custodians of the moral north.

- **Legal Anchors:** Immutable legal constraints that govern machine behaviour regardless of context or optimisation. *Legal Anchors* include international law, privacy mandates, and rules of engagement. They ensure that adaptation never becomes lawless.

- **Living Data Ecosystem:** A dynamic, constantly shifting environment where data is not static information but an active, evolving representation of the world. *Situational Awareness* becomes a shared property of human and machine.

- **Living System / Living Commons:** The evolved form of the *Adaptive Commons*, a system that behaves less like software and more like biology. It eats data, digests patterns, and grows its collective intelligence with every near miss, anomaly, or crisis.

- **Maverick Protection:** The governance principle that preserves outlier insights, unconventional tactics, and creative deviations. *Maverick Protection* ensures that the *Adaptive Commons* does not overwrite human ingenuity in its pursuit of optimisation.

- **Metabolic Advantage:** The defining competitive edge of the hybrid age. *Metabolic Advantage* is the ability of a system, or a civilisation, to absorb shocks, extract insight, and rewrite its operating logic faster than failure can propagate. It is the speed of learning, not the speed of computation.

- **Meta-Doctrine:** The operating system for rules. *Meta-Doctrine* does not define what the rules are; it defines how the rules change. It governs update triggers, authority negotiation, and the integration of the *Third Logic* into standard practice. *Meta-Doctrine* ensures coherence in uncertainty and anchors adaptation to human values.

- **Micro-Decision Space:** The domain of rapid, granular decisions that occur faster than human cognition can track. In this space, the machine operates at full tempo while the human sets intent and ethical boundaries.

- **Micro-Judgements:** The tiny, often unconscious decisions experts make under pressure. These are the fingerprints of adaptive expertise captured by the *Adaptive Commons*.

- **Minority Report Trap:** The term echoes the dilemma explored in Philip K. Dick's 'Minority Report', where predictive certainty leads to pre-emptive action that undermines human agency. Here, the ethical danger of acting on predictions in ways that pre-empt human agency or dignity. The *Minority Report Trap* emerges when foresight becomes pre-emption, when the system removes a human from a role because they might fail.

- **Mission Constraints:** Human-defined ethical and tactical boundaries that shape machine recommendations. *Mission Constraints* ensure that machine optimisation remains aligned with human intent.

- **Moral Debrief Protocol:** A structured post-action process that uses the *Cognitive Trace* and *Reasoning Trace* to help humans process the ethical and emotional impact of hybrid decisions. The goal is not legal defence but psychological integration, moving from unexplained guilt to informed acceptance.

- **Moral Fatigue:** The cumulative ethical load created by repeated exposure to 'least-worst' decisions at machine tempo. *Moral Fatigue* erodes ethical resilience not through catastrophe, but through repetition, the slow wearing down of the human's capacity to care at speed.

- **Moral Residual:** The ethical and emotional 'exhaust' left behind after a high-stakes hybrid decision. The machine resets instantly. The human does not. *Moral Residual* is the weight the system cannot carry, the part of the decision that lingers in memory, conscience, and identity.

- **Narrative Input:** A failure, deviation, or improvisation inside XR that becomes a data input for updating *Meta-Doctrine*. In the hybrid age, failure is not a reset, it is a story the system learns from.

- **Negotiated Authority:** The dynamic exchange of control between human and machine based on conditions, confidence, and context. Authority is no longer fixed; it flows. *Negotiated Authority* ensures that leadership adapts to the moment rather than the manual.

- **Non-Linear Escalation:** A rapid, exponential amplification of instability triggered by the interaction of multiple cycles or forces. It is the moment when a system shifts from manageable to catastrophic.

- **OODA Loop:** Developed by Colonel John Boyd, a United States Air Force fighter pilot and military strategist, the Observe, Orient, Decide, Act Loop is the traditional model of human decision-making. In the hybrid age, the loop fractures under machine-tempo conditions, dissolving into blur and requiring a new cognitive architecture.

- **Persistent Expertise:** The ability of the *Adaptive Commons* to capture the tacit wisdom of experts, their *Friction Signatures*, *Micro-Judgements*, and *Third Logic* patterns, and preserve it beyond the individual. Expertise becomes a persistent property of the system, not a fragile attribute of a single mind.

- **Persistent Simulation Ecosystem:** A living simulation environment that never resets. It evolves continuously based on real-world data, human behaviour, and doctrinal updates. The ecosystem becomes a parallel universe where rehearsal and reality feed each other in a recursive loop.

- **Phase Synchronisation:** A specific failure vector where two independent cycles, mechanical, biological, financial, accidentally align, triggering *Non-Linear Escalation*. The *Adaptive Commons* watches for synchronisation, not for the specific components involved.

- **Positive Feedback Oscillation:** A reinforcing loop that accelerates instability. When a system's corrective actions amplify the problem, oscillation becomes the engine of collapse.

- **Precursor Signature:** The early instability pattern that appears before a failure manifests. A *Precursor Signature* is the shadow of a crisis, the faint tremor in the system that reveals what is coming long before the human can feel it.

- **Predictive Resilience:** The system's ability to anticipate failure before it occurs by recognising *Precursor Signatures* across domains. *Predictive Resilience* transforms failure from a surprise into a signal, enabling hybrid teams to act before the crisis takes shape.

- **Reasoning Trace:** The visible logic path behind a machine's recommendation. The *Reasoning Trace* reveals not just the conclusion, but the steps, assumptions, and thresholds that produced it.

- **Responsibility Gap:** The ethical void created when machine inference influences human action without clear boundaries of agency or intent. The *Responsibility Gap* emerges when the human becomes a passive executor of machine logic rather than the *Final Integrator* of meaning and consequence.

- **Safe Operating Envelope:** The boundary within which a system can function without catastrophic failure. *Divergence Velocity* measures how quickly the system is escaping this envelope.

- **Sanctioned Improvisation:** A deliberate deviation from doctrine driven by human intuition. *Semantic Relational Mapping* recognises this as a signal of opportunity, not error. *Sanctioned Improvisation* is the *Delta of Genius*, the moment when the human sees something the system has not yet processed.

- **Sanctioned Improvisation Zone:** A bounded space within live operations where the human can deviate from machine recommendations without breaking doctrine. In the *Active Zone*, *Sanctioned Improvisation Zones* recognise improvisation as a peak expression of human adaptive expertise where creativity and caution collide.

- **Second Voice:** The moment the machine speaks without being asked, offering an opinion, a contradiction, or a warning based on patterns invisible to the human. The *Second Voice* marks the end of the passive machine and the beginning of the *Cognitive Partnership*.

- **Semantic Feedback Loop:** The real-time calibration cycle through which the machine checks its interpretation of human intent. It is not surveillance; it is synchronisation. The loop ensures that the machine's mental model remains aligned with the human's lived reality, closing the gap between inference and intent.

- **Semantic Relational Mapping (SRM):** The architecture that allows a machine to understand not just what a human does, but why they do it. *Semantic Relational Mapping* transforms behaviour into signal, signal into meaning, and meaning into *Shared Intent*. It is the Rosetta Stone of hybrid teaming, the mechanism that turns human intuition and machine inference into a shared cognitive space.

- **Semantic Sabotage:** An attack that poisons the *Adaptive Commons* by feeding it false patterns, staged failures, or manipulated signals. *Semantic Sabotage* shifts the system's understanding of reality until it learns the wrong lessons with absolute confidence.

- **Sensor Integrity:** A condition within *Conditional Acceptance* that ensures the data streams remain uncompromised. When *Sensor Integrity* drops, autonomy halts, not because the human overrules the machine, but because the machine steps back.

- **Sensory Decoupling:** The separation between human senses and operational reality. Threats now exist in frequencies, packets, and patterns the human nervous system cannot perceive. Machines become the new sensory organs of the hybrid team.

- **Shared Choice Trauma:** The psychological injury that arises when a human accepts or negotiates a machine's recommendation and later questions whether the decision was truly theirs. *Shared Choice Trauma* is the emotional residue of co-decision, guilt without full agency, responsibility without full control.

- **Shared Conscience:** The emergent moral state created when human intuition and machine inference co-author a decision. A *Shared Conscience* is not a merging of minds, but a merging of consequences, a space where responsibility becomes collective even when experience remains human.

- **Shared Intent:** The alignment of goals, meaning, and direction between human and machine. *Shared intent* is the compass of hybrid teaming, the point where both partners move with a unified purpose.

- **Shared Meaning:** The *Cognitive Alignment* that allows human and machine to interpret the world through a common frame. *Shared Meaning* is the foundation of hybrid trust and the precursor to the *Third Logic*.

- **Shared Pulse:** The synchronised cognitive rhythm between human and machine. It is the moment when both are adapting to the world, and to each other, in real time. The *Shared Pulse* becomes the mechanism by which tacit expertise is captured and transformed into *Persistent Expertise*.

- **Shared Reality:** The high-fidelity mental model co-constructed by human and machine through *Semantic Relational Mapping* and the *Semantic Feedback Loop*. *Shared Reality* is the cognitive terrain where the *Third Logic* emerges, a space where both partners see the same world, speak the same language, and move toward the same intent.

- **Silent Signature:** A micro-pattern of instability or threat too faint for human perception but instantly recognisable to the machine through *Semantic Relational Mapping* and *Failure Vector Blueprint* matching. A Silent Signature is the whisper of a crisis before the world knows it exists.

- **Situational Awareness:** A refined meaning and no longer the human's ability to perceive the environment, but the team's ability, human and machine together, to maintain a coherent picture of a world too fast and too complex for either to understand alone.

- **Soft Override:** A subtle, non-intrusive warning issued when the system predicts a high-risk future state. A *Soft Override* preserves human agency while illuminating risk.

- **Solo Adaptation:** The legacy model of human-only decision-making. It is the heroic myth of the individual expert navigating complexity alone, a model that collapses under the velocity of the modern world.

- **Sovereignty of Intent:** The principle that the human remains the final arbiter of meaning in a hybrid team. *Semantic Relational Mapping* does not predict or control the human; it aligns and empowers them. *Sovereignty of Intent* ensures that the *Third Logic* emerges through choice, not coercion.

- **Strategic Presence:** The human's ability to remain grounded, ethical, and intentional while the machine operates at machine tempo. *Strategic Presence* is the anchor that prevents speed from becoming recklessness.

- **Structural Integrity:** Integrity of the hybrid bond is the resilience of the human–machine partnership under stress. *Structural Integrity* is revealed when *Synthetic Friction* pushes the team to its breakpoint, exposing where trust holds, where it fractures, and how it repairs itself.

- **Structural Transparency:** The architectural requirement that the machine's reasoning, assumptions, and decision pathways remain visible and interrogable. *Structural Transparency* is the antidote to blind trust, the window into the machine's mind.

- **Symbiosis (Hybrid Symbiosis):** The state in which human and machine cognition adapt to each other in real time. *Symbiosis* is not harmony; it is co-evolution, the dynamic interplay that produces the *Third Logic*.

- **Symbiotic Upgrade:** The co-evolutionary loop in which humans and machines refine one another's strengths. The *Symbiotic Upgrade* is not replacement, it is mutual enhancement, a recursive ascent in capability and understanding.

- **Synchronisation Trap:** A cross-domain failure mode where two rhythms lock into destructive alignment. It appears in reactors, markets, and human physiology, different skins over the same skeleton.

- **Synthesis Phase:** The process that transforms friction into faculty, converting a single team's crisis into global learning within hours. The *Synthesis Phase* collapses the generational delay of expertise.

- **Synthetic Friction:** Engineered uncertainty injected into XR to test the *Structural Integrity* of the hybrid bond. *Synthetic Friction* introduces ambiguity, stress, and degraded environments, the cognitive equivalent of resistance training, revealing how the team behaves at the edge of failure.

- **Systemic Adaptivity:** Adaptation that emerges not from individuals but from the system as a whole. It is the shift from local learning to global learning, where a lesson learned anywhere becomes a lesson applied everywhere.

- **Systemic Burst Signature:** A dynamic pattern indicating imminent catastrophic failure across any domain. A *Systemic Burst Signature* is the universal signal of a system approaching terminal pressure.

- **Systemic Hallucination:** A large-scale misinterpretation propagated through the *Adaptive Commons* due to poisoned learning inputs. A hallucination becomes systemic when every node inherits the same false belief.

- **Systemic Immortality:** The condition in which organisations, and eventually societies, learn faster than they break. *Systemic Immortality* does not mean systems cannot fail; it means they cannot fail the same way twice.

- **Systemic Metabolism:** The biological process by which the *Adaptive Commons* consumes raw data, digests it into *Failure Vector Blueprints*, and distributes the corrective 'nutrient' across all nodes. It is the metabolic engine of hybrid civilisation.

- **Tactical Flow (Machine Domain):** The machine's ability to manage high-tempo execution while keeping the *Human-in-the-Loop* at the altitude of meaning. *Tactical Flow* is the machine's contribution to hybrid synchrony.

- **Third Logic:** The decision pathway that emerges when human intuition and machine inference synthesise into a single course of action. In ethical contexts, the *Third Logic* is not just a cognitive synthesis, it is a shared moral commitment.

- **Traceability Map:** A transparent lineage of how the system derived its insight, the mathematical DNA that links a warning to its origin. It allows humans to trust a signal even when its source lies outside their domain.

- **Training Paradox:** The central challenge of hybrid training: how to teach a human to trust a machine that contradicts them. Trusting a machine when it agrees is easy; trusting it when it challenges identity is doctrine.

- **Translation Layer:** The mechanism that strips away domain context and reveals the universal physics of failure. The *Translation Layer* is the connective tissue of the *Adaptive Commons*.

- **Translator of Reality:** A machine that reconstructs the world in forms the human nervous system cannot perceive. In submarines, sonar is the translator of the ocean; in cyber defence, the system is the translator of the invisible battlefield.

- **Transparency Paradox:** The tension between too much machine explanation (overload) and too little (blind trust). The *Transparency Paradox* demands a Goldilocks Zone, a level of reasoning that empowers judgement without drowning the human in cognitive noise.

- **Uncanny Valley of Collaboration:** The psychological discomfort that arises when a machine becomes competent enough to challenge human intuition but not yet integrated into the human's identity as a teammate. It is the liminal zone where expertise feels threatened, ego feels exposed, and the human has not yet learned to trust the machine's way of seeing.

- **Universal Translator of Risk:** The *Adaptive Commons* in its most evolved form, capable of translating a failure in one domain into a warning in another, regardless of sector boundaries.

- **Universal Vector (Blueprint):** The domain-neutral representation of a failure pattern, the physics beneath the profession. A *Universal Vector* is what remains when the system strips away context and keeps only the instability itself.

- **Universal Vector of Failure:** The distilled, cross-sector signature of a failure event, stripped of geography, equipment, and context. It is the pure physics of collapse, shared across the *Adaptive Commons* to inoculate every node.

- **Visual Transparency:** The display of the machine's reasoning in a form the human can intuitively grasp. *Visual Transparency* turns inference into insight, making the machine's logic visible at a glance.

- **XR:** Extended Reality (XR) is an umbrella term that covers all immersive technologies blending the physical and digital worlds, including Virtual Reality (VR), Augmented Reality (AR), and Mixed Reality (MR).

- **XR Substrate:** The cognitive environment where hybrid teaming becomes alive. The *XR Substrate* is not a simulator; it is the shared mental terrain where human and machine rehearse, refine, and evolve their partnership. It is the digital soil in which the *Third Logic* grows.

Index

Terms marked "Definition" refer to entries in the consolidated Glossary of Terms (pages 153–179).

About the Author: Christopher Clift

Christopher is a learning scientist and systems thinker with over three decades of experience designing transformational training ecosystems across aerospace, defence, and technology sectors.

Early in his career, Christopher led a multidisciplinary team in developing award-winning instructional systems for commercial pilots and engineers, advancing original concepts that earned three international innovation awards. Two of the world's largest aviation training providers still use evolved forms of those early models today, serving major airlines globally, more than 20 years on.

Since 2013, he has worked in deep collaboration with the UK's Royal Navy Submarine Service and the broader submarine enterprise, helping to modernise its training architecture by integrating advances in cognitive science, simulation, and adaptive learning design. His work has helped reshape how complex human capabilities are developed and sustained in safety-critical environments.

Christopher's current focus lies at the intersection of learning, autonomy, and AI. He is exploring how AI-driven, personalised feedback, delivered through immersive XR environments, can close critical expertise gaps and accelerate decision-making fluency. His mission: to design systems that don't just inform but adapt; that don't just scale knowledge but forge lasting human capability.

His doctoral path at the University of Strathclyde was interrupted when industrial funding was withdrawn. However, with encouragement from the University and colleagues, he never stepped away from the research. What began as a thesis has since evolved, inevitably growing into the trilogy: *Becoming Adaptive*.

Becoming Adaptive represented the synthesis of that work, a blueprint not just for training the future, but for becoming it.

Built around the *ION Learning Model*, the trilogy examines how humans adapt under pressure, drawing on his work with Project Oracle and the operational ethos of HMS Oracle's role in training submarine commanders, where second chances don't exist. In brief:

> **Part 1** introduces the ION Model, exploring the telemetry of behaviour, adaptive imperatives, and pathways to cultivating individual expertise.

> **Part 2** maps cognitive transformation and simulation logic, translating emotional rebound into design and feedback loops.

> **Part 3** shifts the focus to teams and systems, applying adaptive intelligence to leadership development within XR environments.

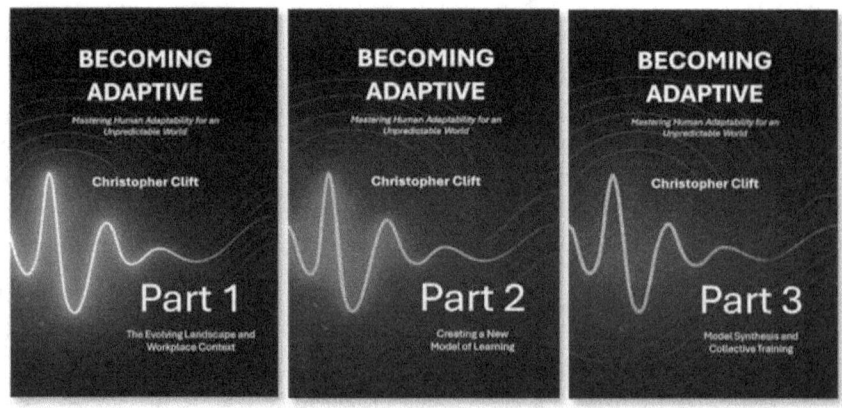

Beyond Adaptive: The Evolution of Human–Machine Teams isn't just a continuation; it's the next frontier of the ideas already established in the *Becoming Adaptive* trilogy.

For the latest updates: https://www.c3connect.co.uk/becoming-adaptive

www.ingramcontent.com/pod-product-compliance
Lightning Source LLC
Chambersburg PA
CBHW070321240526
45468CB00025B/1258